Nostalgic
Wirral

Edited by Pauline Black

The publishers would like to thank the following companies for their support in the production of this book

Main Sponsor
Darlington Group plc

Associated Octel Company Limited

Birkenhead Markets

Deeside Services

Gordale Nurseries

The Grange Shopping Centre

James Heaney & Company Limited

Kingsmead School

D Morgan plc

Pyramids Shopping Centre

First published in Great Britain by True North Books
England
HX5 9AE
Telephone: 01422 377977
© **True North Books Limited 2000**

ISBN 1 903204 15 1

Text, design and origination by True North Books Limited
Printed and bound by The Amadeus Press Limited

Nostalgic Wirral

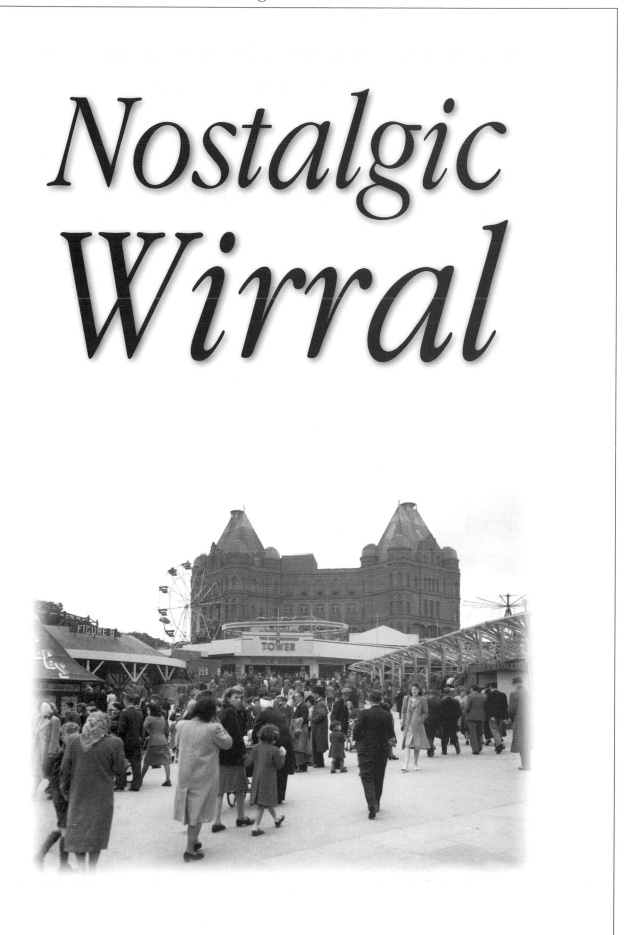

Contents

Introduction

Welcome to 'Nostalgic Wirral'. You are about to embark on a journey of nostalgia that will take you back in time to the music of Billy J Kramer, the films of Mary Pickford, the times of the Lever brothers and the magnificence of Cammel Laird. Thanks to the wonders of photography, the days that are just out of reach of our own memory have been preserved. Nearer to hand are the images of the days through which we have lived. Each superb photograph will bring back to life the days of Wirral that we think we can remember so well. On some occasions the reader will be able to resolve a long dispute about where a certain building actually stood. Other pages might prove that the memory has played tricks.

But, the camera does not lie. Only our mental databanks have faults. Each of the photographs is accompanied by an informative caption. Some add to what we know, some reinforce what we knew. Others might bring a quiet smile to a face that has been there before. Whatever the reaction, there is something for everyone in this book. The more senior of us have been there, the younger audience has heard about it. So that was what grandma wore in her youth and did mum really have her hair in that beehive style? And she has the nerve to criticise the way we dress these days! There are fine buildings to remember that once stood proudly where the modern developer has now had his way. Have the planners improved our lot or have they ruined our heritage? 'Nostalgic Wirral' will start as many arguments as it settles.

The book is not intended to be a history of the region. It is an unleashing of nostalgia that has lain pent up within us all. But, we need to know something of our past to understand more fully our present and plan for the future. We know that Stone Age man was here, perhaps over 5,000 years ago, from fragments of tools that have been unearthed.

The Woodside ferry building and bus station in a picture dating from 1954

M an developed from the prehistoric hunter-gatherer to a more domesticated style of life as a cereal and livestock farmer. During the Bronze Age the Cornovi occupied Wirral. This powerful Celtic tribe was also prominent in Wales and dominated the area for over 1,000 years until the coming of the Romans. Even they preserved the Celtic links by naming the province that was centred at Wroxeter in Shropshire as Cornovii. The Romans arrived on Wirral around 70 AD. They had a large settlement at Meols. They left Wirral behind some 350 years later. The next invasion came from the Vikings who settled along the western side of the peninsula in the 9th century. When the Domesday Book recorded it in the late 11th century, there was a population of about 2,000. Today that figure is nearer to 335,000.

Wirral was almost all an agricultural area until the early 19th century, but with the growth of Liverpool, parts of the peninsula became desirable residential areas for Liverpool businessmen. In 1824 William Laird founded the shipyards at Birkenhead and laid out the town on a grid pattern with Hamilton Square as the focus. Later in the century the Birkenhead docks developed a trade independent of Liverpool. Today industries include flour milling, the manufacture of margarine and pharmaceuticals and marine engineering. The long-established Unilever soap works at Port Sunlight adjoin the model garden village created for employees by the first Lord Leverhulme. The western part of the peninsula dominated the maritime traffic for three centuries. But, as the Dee silted up, Liverpool grew in importance as a major port and international trader. Modern developments have seen international links forged by Wirral docks in more recent times.

New Brighton Tea Gardens in 1950

Hoylake's Market Street on 12th February 1935

Wallasey in a picture dating from the late 1950s

Birkenhead has emerged to take its place as an important shipping centre. However, as with many areas in Britain, it was the coming of the age of rail that helped Wirral first expand in a large way. The first under-water railway, linking Liverpool and Birkenhead, opened in 1886. People and industry poured in and life on the Wirral was to change for ever. But our region is a wonderful place of contrasts. There is the busy life of Birkenhead, with its shopping malls, galleries, commerce and a waterfront of ferries and historic warships. Then we have the fresh sea breezes of the promenades at Hoylake, New Brighton and West Kirby. We can visit Wirral Country Park or stroll the cliffs above the Dee estuary. Then, having returned to our homes along motorway spurs, flyovers and past the facades of buildings that once knew a different life, we can remind ourselves of how it used to be.

Crosville Bus Station, Heswall in the 1950s

The reader now has the chance to start a journey through history that needs neither Tardis nor time capsule. Inside the covers of 'Nostalgic Wirral' is a feast of yesteryear. Babies were pushed along in Silver Cross prams. We collected Green Shield stamps and saved cigarette cards with Denis Compton on them. Our parents worked in the munitions factories and counted their wages in shillings and pence. They were the days of hiding behind the sofa when the rent man came to call and rally-o played in the streets with tin cans and a tennis ball. George Formby and Gracie Fields entertained us on film and on the halls. Sherbet fountains, bullseyes and gobstoppers were a youngster's delight. Dads took lads to the Prenton Park and passed them down to the front, collecting them in safety at the final whistle. Girls played two ball and mums tried out the Wirral version of Dior's New Look as they queued for their meat ration. Pour yourself a glass of Vimto, reach for a packet of Payne's Poppets and light up a Craven A. It is time to start along the nostalgic road as you turn the first page.

Street scenes

Above: Birkenhead. The train has just arrived at Hamilton Square Station. The camera was looking across at the crowded scene from the direction of Woodside Bus Station. It was appropriate that a bus should be the vehicle pictured on this day. Around 1950, all traffic could travel freely along this stretch of road. It is now part of the one way system and a 'bus only' lane, as well. That was one of officialdom's efforts to free up the town streets from congestion. The fashions of the middle of the 20th century are fun to look at. The bowler hatted man is obviously 'something in the city'. Other men have hats, too, but the majority was bareheaded. Before the war it was unusual to see the top of a man's head. Women held onto their hats a little longer. It was part fashion and part modesty. Younger ones did away with convention, but their mothers still thought it unladylike to go out without a hat.

Above right: Birkenhead. The older couple, making its way from Hamilton Square Station in about 1950, has seen plenty of change in their lifetime. He looks dapper in his bow tie as he takes her arm and strides off into the second half of the 20th century. They were born when Queen Victoria was on the throne. In their lifetime they had seen the introduction of the motor car and the first aeroplane, radio, cinema and the new wonder of television had come to entertain them. Two world wars had come and gone and powerful new medicines and drugs made life healthier for them. Behind them, people crossed at the sign of the Belisha beacon. Some of the inventions brought dangers and the zebra crossing was a road safety measure brought in to help pedestrians. The flashing yellow orb was named after Leslie Hore-Belisha, the minister of transport from 1934 to 1937. Above the passengers' heads, Mersey Railways sent out a message, 'Trains every few minutes'. If only rail travel was that reliable today. Ever since Dr Beeching cut the services in the 1960s, we have suffered delays and cancellations that would cause a saint to swear. The railway came to the Wirral long before our couple was born. The first journey was made in 1840 by a locomotive named 'Wirral'. The journey to Chester took just 50 minutes. Fares were expensive. There were three classes of travel, costing one, two or three shillings respectively.

Below centre: Birkenhead - Charing Cross. This area is now virtually unrecognisable, even though shoppers walk across here in droves every day. If you were told that McDonald's fast food shop is on the right and the Pyramids centre is around the corner, then it becomes clearer. This is Charing Cross. The camera has been pointed towards Atherton Street. The roundabout did more than let traffic turn around it. The centre lamp standard had a beacon on top. It flashed for 24 hours following any fatal accident. It acted as a road safety reminder and as a request for help from any witnesses. It was in the 1960s that plans were made to redevelop this area. A new precinct was centred around Grange Road. Much of it was pedestrianised. The large chains moved into many of the new shops. The Pyramids shopping centre gave us covered shopping and parking to make life easier. What we lost was the individuality that this spot once had. Every town centre has the same names on its shops. They all have pedestrianised areas and multi storey car parks. What few of them have kept is that little something to preserve a sense of identity. This view from Charing Cross was definitely Birkenhead. A picture taken of the same place after the developers had their way could be almost anywhere. There is nothing to distinguish it from any other centre.

Bottom: Birkenhead - Grange Road West. This 1930s view of the road towards its junction with Whetstone Lane and Exmouth Street, at Charing Cross, offers some fascinating 'then and now' contrasts. The premises on the far right, which in later years came to be occupied by Irwin's Grocers, have now completely gone. The property on the far left, where Eastbourne Road cuts across, is very recognisable today, along with the rather fine stonework which forms a feature of the upper storeys along the left of Grange Road West. Of the two clocks visible along the right-hand side of the road, only the one in the far distance remains. A stroll along this pavement now, past Clayton Street, would bring you to the old church building which presently houses the Carlton Little Theatre. The 1930s photograph shows that this building appears to still have its tower or spire. Paradoxically, these 1930s shoppers would find it both easier and more difficult on Grange Road now. The volume of traffic is much greater at this end than it was in those far off days, but beyond the Charing Cross junction there is now the luxury of pedestrianisation.

Birkenhead. Not the loveliest of sights in 1961, as the rows of terraced houses sweep down to the docks and gantries of Cammell Laird along the Mersey waterfront, but one that had meant so much for the economic life of Birkenhead and the Wirral. It had been 137 years earlier, in 1824, that William Laird had founded the Birkenhead Iron Works at Wallasey Pool. Laird, an enterprising Scottish businessman, was a man with an eye for the main chance. He had realised that with the Liverpool docks full to capacity, but the Cheshire bank of the river undeveloped, here were distinct possibilities.

William Laird was joined by his son, John, and in 1828 at their new shipyard the first iron ship was built, the 'Wye', a lighter for the Irish Inland Steam Navigation Co. The land purchased by William Laird in Wallasey proved to be an excellent investment, for in 1858 he was able to sell it at a handsome profit to the newly formed Mersey Docks and Harbour Board, and the Lairds moved to a new site between Monk's Ferry and Tranmere Pool. In 1903 an amalgamation with Charles Cammell, a Sheffield based steel manufacturer, created the company that would become internationally renowned as builders of some of Britain's greatest ships.

Right:
Birkenhead - Market Place South. Even 40 years ago traffic congestion was a pain. Gridlock is not a recent invention. As motoring became more popular, town centres paid the price. Drivers saw no reason to

Ellesmere Port Collection

lanes and pedestrian only areas, 21st century traffic is still a problem and the pictured scene on Market Place shows how some things never alter.

Below:
Birkenhead. Conway Street picks up where

leave their vehicles in the garage. They had bought them and intended to use them. It did not matter that it meant sitting for ages in long traffic jams. Lorries came through the town centre and added to the pollution and delay. Market Place South was typical of a scene repeated on other Birkenhead streets every day of the working week. The old market stood to the left of the parked cars where Westminster House council offices now stand. The buildings close to the head of the queue form part of the Hamilton Quarter that is a Wirral arts organisation, set up with the help of European funding. Most of the local public services can date their origins back to 1833. The First Improvement Act brought in measures for paving, lighting and cleansing the streets. It also permitted a market to be established. Francis Price donated the land for it. He would have been happy to see the horses pulling the carts with produce for market. Quite what he might have thought of lorry loads and lines of saloons is another matter. Even with ring roads, bus

Park Road North leaves off, and heads straight as an arrow for the heart of the town. This sunny 1960 scene gives several indications of belonging to another era. The butcher's boy has left his bike casually leaning against a lamp standard, reminiscent of a time when many a meat delivery was made by pedal power. The Alexandra Garage is a reminder too of a time when most garages were on a human scale, a place where you bought your petrol as well as having your car repaired. You could chat to the proprietor, who often appeared from beneath a car to serve you, but you would have got a very strange look indeed if you had tried to pay with a bit of plastic, and asked for some crisps and a newspaper as well! The star of the show at the Alexandra garage in 1960 would undoubtedly have been the Morris Minor. Developed by designer Alexander Issigonis, it was the first all-British car to sell more than a million. Along with the Mini, it became an icon of the dawning car age, and no doubt some readers nervously took to the wheel for the first time in one or the other.

region of £8 million. The rise of mass car ownership from the 1950s brought pressure for a second tunnel and the first tube of the Kingsway Tunnel, running to Wallasey, was opened by Queen Elizabeth II in 1971. The whole tunnel was finally opened in 1973. As for the first tunnel, the Approaches Scheme of 1964 which separated local and tunnel traffic, has altered this 1950 view beyond all recognition.

Top: Birkenhead. Hamilton Square is a visual and architectural gem in the heart of Birkenhead, and is considered to be one of Europe's finest enclosed spaces. It is also a demonstration of the fact that nineteenth century entrepreneurs often left more than just an industrial legacy, for the building of the Square was financed by William Laird,

Above: Birkenhead - Queensway Tunnel. A sprinkling of 'period' advertisements gives a 1950s feel to this photograph, as does the line of rather antique looking wagons emerging from the Birkenhead side of the Queensway Tunnel. Towards the left, the toll-booths are clearly visible. Work on this particular road tunnel beneath the Mersey had begun in 1925, when the growing volume of motor vehicles was proving too much for the ferries. A committee under Sir Archibald Salvidge had considered a bridge, but the members had rejected this because it would have made such an obvious target in the event of another war. Tunnelling took place from both banks of the river, and in 1928 the historic moment came when the two teams broke through to each other. The Lord Mayor of Liverpool, Miss Margaret Beavan, and the Mayor of Birkenhead, Alderman Naylor, shook hands deep below the river. The Queensway Tunnel was opened by King George V in 1934, having cost in the region of £8 million.

the founder of the Birkenhead shipbuilding company, and named after his wife's maternal ancestors. Gillespie Graham designed the layout, and the building period stretched from 1826 to the 1850s. This view was captured in 1959, and the main impact is provided by the wonderful expanse of greenery and gardens intersected by pleasant walkways. The background is dominated by the Classical frontage and domed clock tower of the Town Hall, opened in 1887 by John and William Laird, grandsons of the founder of the Square. This building, along with the houses of Hamilton Square, was constructed from the locally quarried white Storeton stone. The Town Hall ceased to be an administrative centre in 1974 and now houses the Wirral Museum, whilst the Hamilton Quarter is part of the Birkenhead Heritage Trail. Meanwhile the statue to John Laird, Birkenhead's first MP, stands modestly to the far left, although it was originally much nearer the Town Hall.

Birkenhead. Jockeying for position, the lanes of traffic head for the entrance to the tunnel that will take them into Liverpool. The men in the booths were weighed down with cash by the time the day was done. The Mersey Tunnel was a success that created its own problems for Birkenhead. Traffic queued all the way along Market Place South at peak times, blocking movement on neighbouring streets as it tailed back. In later years, sensible tunnel-only lanes were introduced to help town traffic move a little more freely. On the wall of the market, Capstan cigarettes were being advertised on the hoardings. To trumpet recommendations for

poisoning your system seems to be a strange way for mankind to behave. The first market on Hamilton Street was designed by John Jackson. Measuring 180 feet by 90 feet, it stood behind the Town Hall and police station. It had 25 shops and a large number of stands. A new market was opened in 1845 and the old one knocked down in 1888. This covered market was erected in 1909. Passing it by, was a little bubble car, an icon of the 1960s. Popular for a while as a runabout, the driver entered through the front. They looked fragile and no match for a heavier vehicle in an accident. They, like the market, which burned down, are now just history.

Liverpool Libraries & Information Services

East. Only later would we discover the brutal conditions in which many of them had been kept, working on such infamous projects as the Burma railroad. The war memorial, erected in 1925, would need further names adding to it. It would be a roll of honour, but also one of sadness.

Top: Birkenhead. The long descent of Argyle Street South to Birkenhead Central Station, as seen in the 1950s, is instantly recognisable today. However, in many

Above: Birkenhead - Hamilton Square. On a peaceful early autumnal day, there are people dotted around on park benches chatting casually. It is not something they have readily done for over six years. Peaceful days have been few and far between. It is 21 September 1945. The war has only been over for little more than a month. Germany surrendered in May, but it was not until August that victory over Japan was ensured. An air strike over Hiroshima by the American B-29 Enola Gay, followed by an attack on Nagasaki, brought the world into the age of the atom bomb. The Japanese Emperor quickly laid down his sword to save his people further destruction. Many of his traditional warriors felt he should have fallen on it. The bunting, swaying in the breeze above Hamilton Square, was left over from the celebrations of VJ Day. Crowds cheered the speech makers and everyone danced and sang well into the night. Street parties were held and any passing soldier was given a grateful kiss. But, there was still work to be done. There were POWs to be released from the prison camps in the Far

respects there has been a great deal of change, much of it being prompted by the traffic congestion at peak hours that was already being experienced on the roads leading to the Queensway Tunnel. Hence the Tunnel Approaches Scheme, opened in 1964, which separated town traffic from tunnel traffic. The building of the flyover at the bottom end of Borough Road, coming in from the left to the centre, was to lead to the clearance of much of the older property in that area which is visible in the picture. Even the domed memorial to Edward VII, which had stood on the same spot since its erection in 1911, suffered the indignity of being shunted aside by the force of progress. However it did survive, coming to rest in its present position in front of the Central Hotel, with the George and Dragon Hotel to the right. The present view from this elevated position takes in not only the flyover and the Approaches Scheme, but also the radical new skyline on the far side of the Borough Road which has been created by the Grange and Pyramid Shopping Centres.

Liscard Road, or the A551, forges its way out of Liscard amidst pleasant surroundings along the edge of Central Park before transforming itself into Borough Road in Seacombe. As the direct link between the two areas it carries heavy traffic flows, particularly at peak times, rather a contrast to this relaxed scene at Liscard Roundabout in 1948. One solid looking vehicle of the time makes its ponderous way around the roundabout, whilst pedestrians seem to be ambling across the road in a fairly casual manner. How different from today, when crossing at a point such as this requires either a death-

defying sprint or the patience to wait for the little green man. Of course 1948 was a decade before the rise of mass car ownership really began. There was little spare money about in these difficult post-war years, and there was a shortage of steel amongst many other things. The government directed steel towards car makers, who would build cars for export. Not only this, if you did own a car the government had introduced a road vehicle tax in 1947 - at a 'crippling' £1 per year! The very famous Burton's sign was a familiar landmark in many towns and cities at this time, along with a distinctive building style.

Above: Wallasey has had its peaceful moments. This must have been one of them. On a quiet summer day the Valentine & Sons postcard showed the village as we would all like to remember it. Shop awnings had been pulled down to protect the goods on display from the sun. Faded lines would not sell. Food needed protecting from the strong rays because this was in the days before refrigerated display counters . Housewives went from shop to shop along the street buying groceries. Often, the process would be repeated several times during the week. Fridges did not become standard household appliances until the 1960s. Before then, houses had cool larders that helped keep food fresh, but only for a limited time. Shopping for necessities was a regular outing. Shopkeepers knew their customers and their little whims. They always had time for a chat and to ask about the family and if Johnny had settled in at school. Speak to a checkout girl at a supermarket in this day and age and she will complain of harassment! Unlike many other towns, Wallasey does not have an obvious centre from which other districts fan out. It was once a mixture of tiny villages and hamlets. They were strung out like beads on a rosary. Eventually, Liscard became the accepted centre of Wallasey. However, the parish church is in Wallasey village and the town hall some distance away in Brighton Street, Seacombe.

Above right: Wallasey - Dock Road. Looking west on 16 July 1925 was to see all that was both good and bad about that era. Huge warehouses held stores and equipment for import and export. They had a mountain of wealth kept inside. Lorries drove along the cobbled streets, doing a journey that took a fraction of the time it ever used to by horse drawn carts. Railway lines came into the docks to link with the national network. But, there was a price to be paid for this seeming prosperity. Men had returned from the war with the promise of homes fit for heroes. They did not get them. They did not even get the wages to buy them. Working conditions were still dangerous and unhealthy .The phrase, 'health and safety', had not been invented. Smoke from factory chimneys polluted the air and morale among the working classes was low. Dockers were often at the mercy of the men who did the hiring. They turned up for work and were taken on or turned away by one man's decision. Sometimes, if your face fitted, that was fine. But, if it didn't, that was another day without the means to feed the kids. Pawnbrokers and moneylenders did good business. The day of reckoning was one to be dreaded. Neighbours helped out as best they could, but the future was often as bleak as the outlook on Dock Road.

Liverpool Libraries & Information Services

Right: Hoylake. The old chap outside the Punch Bowl probably had salt in his veins. He had lived by and on the sea all his life. He could remember when he was a young man and Queen Victoria had celebrated her Golden Jubilee. In his day there were great advances in transport. The railways were established, great iron ships sailed out of the docks, motor transport appeared on the roads and people took to the skies in the Wright Brothers' invention. But, he was taken with the scene in front of him. Horses made him long for the days of his youth when hooves beat along the tracks and pathways. Carts laden with produce trundled into market. At night, a horse and cart would find its own way home as the farmer had celebrated too well at the inn. Asleep in the back of the cart, he relied on the noble horse to get him back home. It knew the route well and always managed. The group passing the Punch Bowl does not look the sort to be found flat out on their way back from market. The riders were probably part of Hoylake's horsey set. Theirs was a world of business, land ownership, cucumber sandwiches, 'Anyone for tennis?' and the local hunt. They dressed in their hacking jackets and rode as if they ruled the world. They would have been quite happy to aim a blow with their riding crops at any peasant or a motorist who got in their way. Noel Coward could have written a play about their activities. On 12 February 1935 Britain belonged to the upper middle class.

Below: Hoylake was a pretty and busy coastal town on 12 February 1935. Looking down Market Street, the Punch Bowl Inn dominated the corner. Sadly, it has since fallen victim to yet another road widening scheme that swept away so much of our local history. The very name of the inn suggests a life of select gatherings in distinguished homes. The gentry would have gathered for a cup of warming punch after a good day's hunting, shooting or fishing. In Victorian times it was a focal point for the local community that gathered under its then thatched roof. The Tudor style frontage made it an attractive building well worth a second look. The Punch Bowl had grown in popularity just as Hoylake had done during the 19th century. By the end of the Victorian era the district had become a thriving town and shopping centre. It was the first sizeable settlement along the coast from Wallasey and attracted new residents because of its pleasant environment. Shoppers came in from the outlying hamlets to enjoy Hoylake's facilities. The focus moved from the old cottages of Hoose to the commercial centre of Market Street. Brick town houses replaced the sandstone cottages. The shop fronts were given iron canopies and ornate decorations. the displays reflected the prosperity of the town. A description of the town, written in 1903 by a visitor, remarked, 'How different it is from the scattered, sand buried village that smelt strongly of shrimps'.

Bottom: New Ferry - Bebington Road. There appears to be some rather prominent advertising in this 1952 scene. Guinness and Heinz continue to be national names today, but it is likely that the invitation to buy baby linen and hosiery at Okell's had more of a local basis. It is not just the car that gives an early 50s feel to the photograph, but also the woman in the foreground wearing a headscarf. This item of apparel was to be seen everywhere at this time when women were out shopping, to slowly fade away throughout that decade, along with flat caps for men. Younger men and women preferred the bareheaded look. Both New Ferry and nearby Bebington had become part of important transport routes in the nineteeth century, links that were so essential for the general industrial growth of Birkenhead. The introduction of safe crossings of the Mersey by steam ferry after 1817 allowed New Ferry to develop a service that continued until 1922. Bebington, once two rural hamlets, came more to prominence when the lower village found itself on the route of first the stagecoach traffic, and then the railway line, between Chester and Birkenhead. Bebington was also to furnish locally quarried Storeton stone, hard and white, for some of Birkenhead's finer buildings.

Right: Heswall - Village Road. It is a semi rural and village scene that romantics would love to freeze and keep forever. If anything was typical of England as we would like to have it, this is it. The leaves on the trees are only just beginning to fall and the birds are only just beginning to leave our shores for warmer climes. This is the autumn of 1944. Handcarts and hazy days were a lovely backdrop to the village of Heswall. We are looking at Village Road at its junction with School Hill. At the bottom of the hill there was a chance to get a pint at the Black Horse Hotel, formerly Heswall Hotel. In 1801 it was a small community, boasting just 323 inhabitants. It merged with Oldfield in 1899 and the 1901 census records 2,700 people living here. It was a popular place for the well off to have a holiday home. Overlooking the Dee estuary, it was a charming spot to relax and while away some time. The railway helped make it a favourite. Stations here and at Neston and West Kirby opened up this stretch of the Wirral. The walks across the tops and the scenic panoramas across the river and out to sea all added to the attraction of Heswall and its neighbours. When the railway was completed right round to Seacombe, the well to do made their summer homes permanent. They used rail and ferry to commute to Liverpool. A housing boom in the second half of the last century meant that the separate villages of Thingwall, Pensby, Heswall and Gayton have become joined.

evidence of reaching manhood. 'You're never alone with a Strand' was the sort of television slogan that encouraged the young that it was sociable and a cool thing to do. Earlier posters for Craven A suggested you smoke them 'For your throat's sake'.

Top: Ellesmere Port. Westminster Bridge flyover has taken the place of this access road into the town. The group of pedestrians on the right was making its way under the cattle arch that was a convenient detour for animals in days gone by. It became a safe place for people to use, rather than risk being squashed by the buses on the road. Travelling on the bus 40 years ago was fun for

Above: Ellesmere Port Station. The cyclist has made a flying start from the level crossing. He was able to nip through the gates as they started to open once the train had thundered safely on its way. Like some Formula One racers off the front row of the grid, cyclists delighted in leaving the cars and lorries in their wake. Across the road, the housewives were making their way home from doing the day's shopping. In the mid 20th century it was still the custom for many women to walk or take the bus into town and do a daily shop. Fresh bread and something for tea were usually items that featured regularly on their lists. In the distance, an advert for Wills' Capstan cigarettes had been posted on a gable end. They were an acquired taste; the full strength version could blow your head off. Anyone foolish enough to take a deep drag before he had his breakfast was likely to turn a whiter shade of pale. Stars appeared before his eyes and the senses went reeling. Smoking was advertised as a smart thing to do. It was

children. They collected the ends of ticket rolls from kindly conductors and played odds and evens with their ticket numbers. It was good arithmetic practice, adding up the digits and wagering a penny on the result. They were days when conductresses were called clippies and they cried, 'Hold very tight, please', before ringing the bell and setting us off on our journey. It was great to be on the top deck. You could see for miles. If you were lucky you might be able to peek into someone's bedroom. Who knows what scenes were waiting to be spied upon? The buses spawned popular songs and comedy programmes. The nightclub revue artists Flanders and Swann recorded an amusing ditty about a London Transport 47 horsepower omnibus. ITV had a long running sitcom, 'On the Buses', starring Reg Varney and Stephen Lewis. There is a well known song from the 1960s, 'Big Yellow Taxi', that Joni Mitchell sang. However, Lester's Taxis, on the station forecourt, was not as colourful a firm.

Ellesmere Port Collection

Ellesmere Port Collection

High days & holidays

Above: The neon lights of the Gaumont beamed a welcome to all Birkenhead movie buffs in 1938. Perhaps they were on their way to see Errol Flynn swashbuckle his way through 'The Adventures of Robin Hood' or to marvel at the extravaganza that was a Busby Berkeley film. Hollywood turned out some epics in the 1930s, the first full decade of films that had sound-tracks. Cinema audiences were enthralled with the glamour of 'Tinseltown'. The escapades of the stars were hot news. To see and hear them on the silver screen was a weekly must before the age of television. Greta Garbo and Merle Oberon were firm favourites. How sad the men were when the lovely Mary Pickford, the 'American sweetheart', retired. The Gaumont was once a skating rink, before becoming the Electric Palace in 1911. At 1a Park Road East, the audiences were treated to flick-ering black and white short films. Sound came from the pianist in the auditorium pit. She tinkled the ivories in tune with the action on the screen. Villains were greeted with heavy bass notes and romantic moments with sweeping chords. Little captions popped up on the screen to tell us what was being said or what was happening. For a short while, the Electric Palace ran to something grander than the humble pianist. It had a small string orchestra. Prices varied from twopence to a shilling. At the Saturday matinee, children got a free barley sugar stick. It was demolished in 1937 to make way for this new building, designed by WE Trent. There were plaques of Pierrot, Pierrette and Clown on the facade and it held an audience of 1,694.

A tranquil and relaxing scene in the heart of the Wirral is captured in this shot of Birkenhead Park in 1950. As the sunshine through the leaves dapples the path, mothers and children enjoy the delights of this beautiful picnicking and playing spot. The sturdy prams bear the stamp of that era of half a century ago, but whether it be 1950 or the new millenium there is nothing quite like a day in the park in the sunshine. For mothers it gives the chance to 'recharge the batteries', whilst it serves the opposite purpose for the children - getting rid of some of that surplus energy. What a wonderful legacy was left to the area by the creation of Birkenhead Park in 1847, the first municipal park in Britain. An unpromising stretch of marshland between Claughton and the town centre, around 125 acres, was the raw material for Sir Joseph Paxton to work on. In a moment of inspiration he devised the idea of creating two large lakes for the marsh water to drain into. The spoil from the excavations went to create islands and hillocks which were planted with shrubs and trees. The end result was a thing of beauty for future generations, and a model for later creations, including New York's Central Park.

Huge crowds flocked to Merseyside's own seaside resort, New Brighton, in the years immediately following World War II when people were determined to enjoy themselves after the dark years. This shot of 1948 shows a well-thronged fairground, with the typical fashions of the day, and all the thrills of the 'Figure 8' Rollercoaster or Big Wheel awaiting the adventurous. For others an ice-cream and a visit to the Tower Ballroom and Theatre might have been more to their liking. Although the building is imposing enough, to give it the name of The New Brighton Tower seems to be stretching it a bit. However a

tower once did stand on top of the building, a replica of Blackpool Tower, and standing at 562 feet (as opposed to Blackpool's 518 feet) it was the highest structure in Britain. It was built between 1897 and 1900, at a cost of £120,000. However, maintenance was neglected during World War I, and the tower was demolished on safety grounds between 1919 and 1921. The building beneath continued to host a range of entertainments including musical comedy, dancing and wrestling. It even had its own symphony orchestra in the 1920s under the distinguished musical director, Granville Bantock. The tower building was destroyed by fire in 1969.

Above: For those who live near the sea or at the mouths of great rivers there is a constant fascination with boats and ships. The large liners have that aura of glamour and romance, but even the smallest cargo boat may be carrying something exotic from some faraway, mysterious place. Even miniature boats have their fascination, as this 1962 shot reveals, for a good crowd has gathered at the Boating Lake in New Brighton to see the little vessels put through their paces. The traditional sail boats clearly have their followers, but probably most interest is being generated by the remote control vessel which is being directed by the gentleman in the foreground, to the right. This must have been the last word in 'hi-tec' in 1962! Unhappily the fascination of Wallasey people with boats, large or small, was not always such an innocent one. In the eighteenth century a Royal Commission picked out Wallasey as being second only to Cornwall in the criminal activity of 'wrecking', ie deliberately luring ships into running aground by lighting fires to mislead their captains. Cargoes were plundered, whilst survivors of the wrecks were quickly dispatched. Apparently the wreckers would even 'mutilate dead bodies for the sake of rings and personal ornaments' - desperate people indeed!

Above right: There seems to be plenty of room at the open-air swimming pool at New Brighton in this 1947 photograph, but perhaps the weather was not too hot. The building of municipal baths expanded greatly across Britain in the nineteenth century, along with urbanisation. Local councils became concerned about the numbers of people either drowning or picking up infectious diseases through swimming in canals and rivers. However, a man who might have been surprised at the creation of a swimming pool at New Brighton was James Atherton, the man who founded the place. In 1830 he bought 170 acres of sandhills in order to create a seaside resort to rival Brighton. One of the great advantages he saw was the potential for healthy bathing in the sea. Unfortunately, apart from dangerous tides, it soon became apparent that the sea could become as polluted as any industrial river. In 1850 for example, at nearby Seacombe, a householders' petition complained about the state of the shoreline of Wallasey Pool, filthy with industrial effluent and the outpourings of the drains and sewers of Seacombe. Storms in February 1990 saw the end of the pool due to a staggering £4 million repair bill.

This page: New Brighton's wonderful and popular miniature railway is featured in these two evocative pictures. The first one (below centre), dated at 1949, shows a little tank engine in full steam as it races alongside the promenade. The body of the driver is visible, crouching inside the cab, no doubt feeding the firebox with something like a garden trowel. The second photograph (bottom) captures a much brighter day, this time in 1951, with two engines at rest and the opportunity for a group of young boys to examine the mechanics of the engines. For some the miniature railway was no more than an exciting little ride. For others it was this, plus the chance to marvel at the exact detail and craftsmanship of these small-scale replicas. The background too holds its interest, for at the end of the pier and the ferry

bridge, the funnel of the ferry steamer can be seen. Perhaps for some amongst the stream of people coursing along the promenade, their day out at the seaside was over, and they were heading for the ferry home.

And what a day out visitors to New Brighton could enjoy during this era. Liverpudlians came by ferry, in itself a trip that could have children agog with excitement for days in advance. Then there were the sands, beach minstrels, donkey rides, 'Punch and Judy', the pier, the funfair, the boating lake and the miniature railway, along with every chance to make themselves sick with candy floss, toffee apples and ice-cream - a veritable children's paradise. Adults could join in the fun or opt for the quieter pleasures of the deck-chair and maybe a concert at the Tower Theatre. And yet the New Brighton that gave so many fond memories to the people of Merseyside and the Wirral is virtually gone. By the later 1950s there were complaints that the sand was turning to mud. At about this time the rise of mass car ownership began, and people could travel further afield. Then again there was the advent of the package holiday and, ironically, the first ever package flight took off from Liverpool Airport to the South of France in 1952. Whatever the reasons, the numbers visiting New Brighton began to decline. The ferry was discontinued in 1973 and the main pier was demolished in 1978. What is left is eight miles of promenade, the Floral Pavilion Theatre and some excellent amenities for activities such as ten pin bowling, go-karting, golf and sea and beach sports. New Brighton is a sleeping giant waiting to arise.

Above: The British seaside - 1949 New Brighton style. It doesn't really look like a heatwave, and the young lady in the swimsuit might well have been seeking some protection from the breeze in the sand dunes, but there are still plenty of people in the sea. New Brighton was enormously popular as a holiday spot in the immediate post-war years, and people from Liverpool and the Wirral regarded it as their own playground. If New Brighton had the image of being 'cheap and cheerful', the Wirral's own Blackpool, this was very far from the aim of the man who founded it. In 1830 James Atherton bought 170 acres of sandhills in the hope of building up an exclusive seaside resort, with detached houses in ample grounds, fit for the nobility and gentry. Alas for him, within 50 years New Brighton had become notorious as 'the favourite resort of Liverpool and Lancashire trippers and roughs', with bawdy sideshows and hucksters' stalls, accompanied by drunkenness and brawling along 'Ham and Egg Parade', near the Tower. Firm action by the local council had cleaned the place up by 1905, and New Brighton entered its long heyday as a family holiday resort, only for a sad decline to set in from the late 1950s.

Right: The pier is a great British institution, and many readers will have happy childhood memories of slot machines, 'Punch and Judy' shows, candy floss and the walk along the boards to the very end to enjoy the gusty breezes and watch the sea churning around the supports. For Merseysiders, of course, the recollections of sound, colour and taste might refer to New Brighton Pier, as featured in this picture taken in 1961. The deck-chairs are pretty well occupied for the little pier show that is underway, and judging from the number of reclining bodies at the right-hand side, that must have been the place to catch the sun, for the deck-chairs opposite are practically empty. Other attractions are not far away, including the bar and the cafe to the right, whilst in the background, to the left, the Tower Ballroom and Theatre is visible. No doubt the music and screams from the adjoining fairground had a magnetic allure for the youngsters and the 'young at heart' on the pier. By 1961, however, New Brighton was well past its heyday as a holiday resort, and at the end of the 1972 season the pier was closed, to be demolished in 1978.

Enjoying yourself can be hard work, and after a tramp along the pier and the promenade, with perhaps a foray into the funfair, it would be time to take the weight off your feet. In that case the sight of the Tea Gardens was no doubt very welcome to these New Brighton visitors in 1950, especially the adults. Children, of course are inexhaustible at the seaside, preferring to take in their ice-cream and candy floss rations 'on the hoof' whilst continuing to go on every ride possible. The closeness to the end of World War II is indicated by the presence of servicemen, for there were still plenty about at this date, especially with National Service for young men in operation. Another very interesting sign of the times is, literally, the one saying 'No Food Parcels'. We are accustomed to being requested not to consume our own food in cafes and tearooms, but this sign had specific connotations. Britain was in such dire straits after the end of the war that food parcels continued to arrive in great quantities from the USA and the Commonwealth. Clearly Barbara was determined that none of the contents should be consumed at her Buffet Bar in preference to her wares!

Liverpool Libraries & Information Services

of golf scoring that still bears his name. In between the two wars this was a grand place to promenade. Sweethearts strolled the path above the embankment, arm in arm. Picnics were held down by the water side and children paddled to their hearts' content. Water wings and rubber rings gave confidence to those learning to swim. Girls wore caps to keep their hair dry and men and women both wore one piece bathing suits. Thongs were just pieces of leather in those far off days.

Top: Vale Park in New Brighton, seen here in 1948, was a world away from the donkey rides, the funfair and the general hurly-burly of the sea front and pier. It offered a haven of tranquillity for those who preferred the sound of the birds to the strident tones of the

Above: There was an alternative to sending a Donald McGill postcard. You could always post one of Whitfield & Cannon's own scenes of the beach at Harrison Drive. It was a local Wallasey firm, so you were helping local industry as well. McGill's scenes were of fat ladies and saucy young women. They always had a slightly racy caption that might have been a little too near the knuckle if the card were on its way to a straightlaced Auntie Jessie at home. The sea front at the end of Harrison Drive was a popular spot for splashing around in the waves. The drive led from the village to the end of King's Parade that ran along the coast northeast before joining the Promenade at New Brighton. Close by, to the right of the picture, budding Henry Cottons could enjoy the links at Wallasey Golf Club. It was founded in 1891 when its captain was Dr Frank Stableford. He was the man who invented the form

carousels. Not that music was alien to Vale Park, for the dome of the bandstand is clearly visible, and judging by the cluster of people in its vicinity, perhaps a concert was imminent or in progress. To those who lived through World War II, it must have felt wonderfully liberating to walk in the fresh air and sunshine without the fear of sudden attack from the air, or the worry of having a loved one somewhere in the front line. Then again, the immediate post-war world was not too cheerful a place, with shortages, rationing and restrictions lasting into the 1950s, so people made the best of simple pleasures. Vale Park was an ideal place to relax and 'unwind' - to park the pram and have a little read perhaps. Those old prams certainly looked to be of the 'boneshaker' variety, unlike the luxury, large-wheeled ones which were to swish onto the scene in the following decade.

It's a busy day in 1949 on the sands below Egremont Promenade. All ages are represented, from the very young in prams to those at the other end of the scale in deck-chairs. There's plenty of sport to be had on the beach or where the Mersey is just licking the shore. The day is bright, but judging by the amount of clothing still being worn, not too warm, although in 1949 people did not cast their garments off quite so readily as today. Egremont once had the longest pier on the Mersey. This proud boast could have its disadvantages, as in 1932 when a drifting oil tanker found that the first

obstacle it came up against was the long 'finger' of Egremont Pier, which it badly damaged. Unfortunately a coaster did much the same in 1941, to such a degree that Wallasey Corporation felt obliged to close both the pier and the ferry service. The pier was demolished in 1946, the sole remnant of it being the glass-sided public shelter known as the 'Beehive', which is visible in the background. Egremont itself took its name from a large house owned by one John Askew, who developed the area in the nineteenth century, and named his house after his birthplace - Egremont in Cumbria.

Wartime

Not far from Eastham Ferry, Bebington Council's decontamination squad was hard at work in 1940. Every precaution against real contamination had been taken in what was probably a training exercise. Looking like something out of a sci-fi comic, they donned protective overalls, rubber gloves, wellingtons and gas masks. Not an inch of skin was exposed. People had long memories and the fear of germ warfare or poisoning was never too far away in the first year of the war. These workers' fathers had experienced the damage that gas attacks did in the 1914-18 war. Chlorine gas was used at Ypres in 1915. Allied troops could only use wet cloths pressed to their faces to keep out the deadly fumes. The health of those who survived was ruined forever. But, it was not just one side. Both factions used mustard gas in 1917. In that same dirty war, biological attacks were made. In the United States, German agents infected cavalry horses, as well as livestock in a shipment bound for Britain. They introduced glanders, a disease that could cross from animals to humans, causing horrid ulcers and sores to build up in the lungs. When the second world war began, there was a nagging worry that enemy agents could be active again. Now that technology had moved forward, bombs that contained all sorts of unimaginable horrors could be dropped, releasing their deadly viruses into the air. No wonder that the Bebington squad took its work seriously. Man's inhumanity to man knows no bounds.

Below: This was not the Wirral's answer to the Motor Show. Why is it that pretty girls in swimsuits sell cars and no photographer is content to take a shot of young women without their having to flash a bit of leg? Those behind the camera are always men, as are the motor dealers and the buyers with fat cigars. These lovelies, to use the sort of description a tabloid caption writer would use, will be the great grandmothers sitting in the corner of your lounges as you look at this image. If they tut tut about the antics of the young of this era, remind them of what they were up to 60 years ago. But, that generation of women had a lot more about them than any bimbo draped across the bonnet of a modern car. They answered the call of the nation before it had even been made. The civil defence of our land in World War II was left in the hands of those in essential jobs, the ones too old or too infirm to enlist, the very young and a vast unofficial army of women. They tilled the land, often far from home, and went into the munitions and engineering factories. They joined the Auxiliary Territorial Service and Women's Royal Army Corps. The Red Cross was inundated with volunteers and the Women's Voluntary Service was launched. Brave women putting themselves in mortal danger, all in the nation's cause, supported fire and ambulance services. They braved the bombs and dodged the flames. Their soup wagons avoided the falling rubble from damaged buildings as they brought refreshment to those in the thickest of the action. Burned and injured casualties were treated and whisked off to hospital, despite the dangerous conditions all around. Overseas, women drove ambulances into battle zones and risked life and limb to get the wounded out.

Bottom: The Oval, Bebington is now a leisure centre. In 1939 it was home to a food decontamination squad, formed of local shopkeepers and assistants. Their HQ was a former cattle shed in the Oval grounds. The ARP later used it as a temporary mortuary. Sadly, it had some use. During World War II, German bombing raids left 464 dead, 288 in one dreadful night in March 1941. When Britain prepared to do battle with the enemy, it was not just those who joined the armed forces that carried the fight to Hitler. At home, we all did our bit. Civil defence was everybody's responsibility. The Women's Voluntary Service provided admirable support. People gave time to their community as air raid wardens. Girls joined the Land Army and Local Defence Volunteers (the Home Guard) drilled ready to repel any invader. Auxiliary fire and ambulance crews were formed. Other smaller organisations sprang up. This group of noble individuals was ready to deal with any problems that might affect our food. Fear of contamination, either accidental or deliberate, was a real worry in the war's early days. Britain was in a state of alert. The Bebington food decontamination squad, with its protective clothing and hard hats, was ready for action.

Ellesmere Port Collection

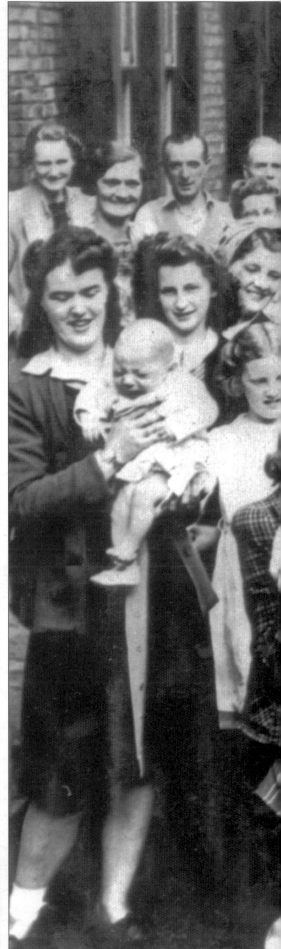

Below: Although newsreels from the Spanish Civil War had given us an idea of what to expect, when the bombs fell in earnest it was far worse than we could ever have expected. How do you prepare for the knot in the stomach as the whine of the bomb on its way to earth makes antici-pation almost as bad as the real thing? Pictures of devas-tation from a foreign shore are not the same as the harsh reality of fire, death and destruction when it hits you personally. The phoney war, when it was quiet at home, was well and truly over. The only surprise was that it had gone on for nearly a year. Then the Luftwaffe left its calling card. Prenton was the first to be hit, on 9 August 1940. Johanna Mandale, a servant girl, was the sad casualty recorded as the first victim. Worse was to come the following month. In September, there were 11 raids. At the time, we wondered when or where it would all end. We rushed off to any of the 7,800 domestic brick shelters that were built. We huddled under the 3,000 Morrison indoor shelters that looked like little igloos. They were probably about as safe. Better were the 6,000 Anderson shelters dug at a cost of £200,000. Deep safehavens at Tranmere Hill and Bidston Hill could hold 9,000 people between them. Here, the scene is of the damage to the 1863 hydraulic tower at Birkenhead Dock. It was a carbon copy of a Florentine building, the Piazza Della Signoria.

Just off Church Road, near Mersey Park, these residents of Hampden Grove are about to have a whale of a time. There are hardly any young men to be seen. They are still waiting to be demobbed. This is to be a party for women, children and grandpas. Celebrations to herald VE Day, when the end of hostilities in Europe was announced on 7 May 1945, were repeated on 14 August for VJ Day. With the victory over Japan secure, we were ready to let our hair down. After nearly six years of trial and turmoil, we could relax. All over the country trestle tables were pulled out onto the pavements. Coloured strips of cloth were hung from lampposts and flags fluttered across window sills. Schoolrooms and church halls lent their tables and benches. Dining room chairs appeared outside the front door and the street parties began in earnest. Neighbours had become even more reliant on each other during the years of deprivation. With rationing biting hard, they helped out with the loan of a cup of sugar or an outgrown frock. Now they were getting together to give their children the time of their lives. Hoarded ration coupons were pooled. Sandwiches were filled, cakes baked in the oven and homemade orangeade appeared as if by magic. The best drawer in the sideboard was raided for tablecloths and excited kiddies sat down and tucked in. Some mums shed a silent tear for the men who would not be coming home, but joined in with the rest to welcome a brighter and better world.

On the road to Wirral

Anyone familiar with Wirral's roads will also be familiar with the name Darlingtons. That name appears on the sides of the firm's fleet of lorries and bulk tippers based at the Group's depots in Eastham and Heswall. And not only does the company name appear on lorries: those who spend their time watching men at work on building sites and excavations around north Wales and the north west of England will not infrequently come across the Darlingtons name appearing on caterpillar tracked diggers and other equipment hired from this ever expanding firm. But where did it all begin?

Arthur Darlington was a farmer's son descended from a long line of yeomen who had farmed and worked the land in and around Northwich for 400 years in such places as Allostock, Marbury Mill, Whitley, Frodsham and Ince. Arthur broke the family tradition and did not follow in his father's footsteps after his father died on the eve of the Great War when Arthur was 17 years old.

After serving in the Household Battalion during the first world war Arthur started a new venture – his own haulage business.

Today the company has a remarkable, reliable, flexible and cost-effective transport and distribution service of high quality provided to a broad client base and includes carriage of raw materials and primary delivery of finished products. In those early days however haulage meant horse transport of which the fledgling firm had several. In 1930 however Arthur Darlington bought his first lorry: a Ford model A, 30 cwt tipper registration number

Above: A letterhead in the 1940s.
Below: Three generations of the family, Arthur, Arthur T and John.

TF 1416 which he bought from the Grosvenor Motor Company in Prestatyn, North Wales for £400.

With today's huge, high-powered, gleaming trucks with air brakes, multiple tyres and massive pulling power it is sometimes difficult to recall just how primitive those early motor lorries were.

The new tipper lorry was no engineering wonder; it was of a simple design - a four cylinder engine, hand operated wiper, rod operated brakes - which were only efficient when the lorry was empty - six volt lighting, hand operated tipping gear and single wheels all round. That tipper lorry was the first of what would eventually grow to today's large fleet of Darlingtons bulk tippers.

Top: *A 1953 Leyland Comet Tipper.*
Above centre: *Mr Arthur snr and employees in 1935.*

Naturally the new business needed somewhere to base itself. The firm's first garage was at the corner of Telegraph Road and North Drive Heswall. The second was on land between Hillside Road and the Ridgeway, land then owned by a Mr Frodsham.

The 1920 and 1930s were not however the best of times for anyone to try and start a new business. The brief economic boom which had followed the cessation of hostilities in 1918 was followed all too soon by recession and 3 million unemployment. Men who had fought in 'the war to end all wars' found work hard to come by and soon discovered that the government had little idea how to tackle the nation's terrible economic ills. Fortunately there was still some work about - even if it was not easy to come by.

Arthur Darlington's main business at that time was daywork for Cheshire County Council in number 9 district. Working conditions in those inter-war days were: 7.00 am start, breakfast at 7.30 until 8 am and no other breaks until 12 noon, 5 ½ days a week.

Dinner was 12 until 1pm and finish was 5.30 pm. There was no travel time back then, the driver had to be on the job at 7.30. No toilets or canteens were available, but a brazier, a kettle and coal were supplied for the hot water. The Council's tender form stipulated that the driver had to work with the outside gang but no protective clothing was made available. Even with overtime the driver's income would not be more than £2 10 shillings (£2.50) per week.

Times were very hard and even though a man might have a job nevertheless in some industries that didn't mean he had a full week's work, in fact in some areas employees were asked to take a reduction in pay.

Supplying turf and soil etc. to local houses, hospitals and market gardens was one way in which Arthur Darlington tried to diversify. Construction work was also undertaken on drives, car parks and tennis courts. Nothing was turned away and no job was too small.

Above: *A Muirhill Loading Shovel and a Leyland Lynx tipper.* ***Top:*** *A 1938 Leyland Lynx.*

Everything that could be moved was carried. One daybook from 1934 reads: 'moving coffin from W J Griffiths, a builder in Telegraph Road to Lower Heswall 5 shillings (50p)'. The daybook does not indicate whether the coffin was occupied or not!

One of the things people take for granted today is the regular weekly arrival of the binmen to empty their dustbins or take away their plastic bin bags. Life was not always so organised, and in some districts such collections were rare or unknown. Nevertheless local authorities were keen to extend such services.

In 1934 when horses were still being used for local work one contract obtained by Arthur Darlington from the local urban council was to empty refuse bins and ash pits with a horse drawn lorry plus a motor lorry - this was long before the advent of wheelie bins. The contract for Heswall cum Oldfield was for £500 per annum and was the first of its kind for homes in Heswall.

Indicative of the hard times and the lengths people would go to for work is the fact that one of the men employed on that refuse removal contract came every day from Liverpool on his bike via the luggage boat across the Mersey and then cycled to Heswall. How many people today would go to such lengths we wonder?

Although the following years saw the worst of the great depression Arthur still managed to expand and bought more tipper lorries and two Aveling-Barford Road Rollers. Arthur's first petrol engined footpath roller cost £283 and 2 shillings; he soon

put it to work for Cheshire County Council and for local builders. That part of the business had developed from the cartage of road and building materials from quarries in North Wales into Wirral and south Lancashire and from doing related daywork for local contractors.

Those who found businesses often seem to be unique characters. One aspect of Arthur Darlington's character and business manner is illustrated by the fact that he would never sign an order or contract for a lorry; he said his word was his bond; if the vendor would not accept that then he could forget the sale. A different facet of Arthur's character is revealed by his never having a new lorry or equipment delivered on a Friday - he much preferred Saturday, when the cheque would be handed over on delivery giving an extra day's grace on payment!

The business continued to grow and in May 1934 became an early member of the Road Haulage Association.

In 1935 the business moved to Downham Road North in Heswall where there were covered premises together with stables for the firm's horses. One cannot help but wonder if even as late as that year whether Arthur Darlington, a man with considerable foresight, could envisage a time when the horse would be just a memory; a time which would come far sooner than most would have predicted.

In the midst of the second world war, in December 1942, the business became a limited company under the formal name of A Darlington (Transport) Ltd.

Above: Two of the company's early advertisements, the top one appearing in Commercial Motor.

The directors of the new company were Arthur Darlington together with his wife Mrs M E Darlington, a lady who would remain on the board until her death in 1995.

During the war years work was undertaken on essential building work and bomb damaged property as well as the maintenance and building of aerodromes such as RAF camp at West Kirby, Sealand, Hooton and Hawarden and the Roften Works alongside Hooton Station. Other important work in this period included maintaining coal supplies to local hospitals. It is perhaps sometimes forgotten just how much the country relied on its transport system in order to keep going when the rest of Europe had collapsed before the Nazi onslaught. Foodstuffs, building materials and, perhaps above all, coal which powered most of industry and in turn fed the war economy were vital ingredients of the long awaited victory of 1945.

After the war loading-shovels and bulldozers were acquired and were hired to local builders, contractors and local authorities. Demand as high in the post war boom in building and

reconstruction. And fortunately that boom unlike that which followed the end of the first world war was not followed by depression and recession. Firms which had survived the bad years now reaped the benefits of the good ones; and Darlingtons did well. Plant hire is today a large part of the Darlingtons business, the firm has now acquired decades of expertise in the hiring out of specialist plant involved in construction, landscaping and industrial projects.

Meanwhile the transport of coal, timber, pit props, animal feeds, oil products and refractories became an important part of Darlingtons' transport business, a business which was set to grow throughout the 1940s and 50s.

The first loading-shovel had been bought in 1949; it was a wire-operated 'Muirhill' driven by a Fordson tractor petrol engine and constructed by Boydell's in Altrincham. The price of that loading shovel was £946 seven shillings and eightpence. A second shovel bought in 1950 cost £978 five shillings and no pence. Today similar equipment hired out by the

Below: *An ERF tractor unit in the 1970s.*

company represents tens of thousands of pounds of investment.

The business changed considerably after 1950 when the company became involved with the transport of industrial coal, refractory materials and bulk materials unloaded from ships at Birkenhead such as fullers earth, solid bitumen and oil in drums.

Business became ever more demanding and loads ever larger. It soon became the company policy to buy ever larger vehicles, moving up from 14 tons to

26 tons Gross Vehicle Weight and beyond to cope with the increase in business in the post war boom. Some of this new work was for companies which had recently opened new works in Wirral such as Morgan refractories, Lubrizol, Shell Star and others.

In March 1963 the company name was changed to A Darlington (Heswall) Ltd.

In the 1960s Arthur Darlington had the foresight to import soil shredding machines from the USA and this remains an activity that is still carried on today. There are usually several thousand tons of soil in stock and shredded soil is therefore always on hand provided the weather is dry. Darlingtons provides soil for a wide range of uses from domestic gardens to major landscaping and development projects. Offering to supply clients with soil is just part of Darlingtons tailor made solutions and project management for both small and large landscaping projects.

From the very beginning soil has been and remains a major part of the business; clients were and still

Above: The fleet in the 1960s.
Left: 1953 Aveline Barford 6 ton roller.

are local authorities, local and national landscape companies. One of the earliest customers for soil was Sir Alfred McAlpine Ltd then working on the new Mersey Tunnel: soil supplied by Darlingtons was used on the approaches to the Birkenhead entrance in 1934. Today, in addition to just soil, the Darlington group also supplies such related materials as garden products available in domestic or industrial quantities - bark, peat and slate. Similarly both households and industrial and development customers benefit from Darlingtons' stocks which include limestone, sandstone and decorative gravels.

Salt in all its forms for all seasons is another product the firm has now been marketing for several years. It is used by farmers for cattle, housewives for dish washers and by local councils for roads.

Does anyone now recall the Darlington Balloon? In the 1970s Mr Arthur T Darlington, the founder's son and chairman since 1967, bought an advertising balloon that was anchored over Heswall: it almost caused several accidents with people driving past watched it rather than the road. Sadly in 1973 Arthur Darlington, the firm's founder, died age 77.

More recently, in 1999, new premises were acquired in Bankfield Drive, Eastham adjacent to the Manchester Ship Canal and near Vauxhall Motors.

The present transport operation is undertaken from that Eastham depot from where several purpose built vehicles work for Cheshire Recycling.

Darlingtons plays a major role in the recycling of waste paper from a variety of locations in the North west including paper banks, super market multi-banks and compactor bins at customer's premises.

Above: *A dockside scene - one of the tall ships in Birkenhead Docks.*

Other Eastham-based vehicle continue to serve existing clients distributing goods throughout the UK. The firm's warehouses, which are situated at Ellesmere port, Deeside and Bromborough, are designed for goods that need racking as well as bulk materials. Indeed the company has built up an excellent reputation in the North West for designing and managing cost effective warehousing and distribution operations. A comprehensive range of services includes wide and narrow-aisled racking in addition to conventional systems.

The road sweeper section of the company now provides equipment to clean factories, car parks and roads in and around North Wales and Merseyside. Darlingtons' multi-function road cleansing equipment is playing a major part in the drive for an improved living and working environment. A fully comprehensive service capable of tackling the toughest challenges includes high pressure cleaning of factory roads and car parks and drain and gully clearing.

Darlington Group PLC's vision is to create a large transport business in north Wales, the North West and the Midlands. It intends to achieve that goal though integrity and trust, and, by being an economic, innovative and environmentally responsible operator, consistently delivering value and quality to its clients.

In 1988 John P Darlington, grandson of the firm's founder, became chairman following the retirement of his father. A fourth generation now works for the firm in the shape of John's daughter Sara who looks after accounts at Eastham, the main transport and warehouse depot and Mandy who is sales manager at the Heswall HQ. Phil Honor is the group's managing director.

John Darlington is now leading the family firm in a programme of expansion and modernisation tuned to the needs of customers in the new millennium. Arthur Darlington would be proud to know that the firm he founded is still in such enthusiastic hands.

Above: One of Darlington's Caterpillar loading shovels. Below: Darlington's Caterpillar 215 excavator.

Bird's eye view

This is a place the Victorian benefactor Joseph Mayer came to love. He settled here in 1864, after a successful business career in Liverpool. An avid traveller and collector, he presented Liverpool Museum with his personal collection, worth several million in today's money. He built the old Bebington Library and his lands became Mayer Park. The aerial view of Bebington, looking east, dates from 10 July 1937. It was taken as a memento of former times. Bebington was to become a municipal borough on 20 August 1937, by order of a royal charter. It grew to a population of 53,000 and had its own Member of Parliament. Its separate identity did not last long in historical terms. In 1974 local government reorganisation allowed Wirral Borough to swallow it up. That was the piece of legislation that gave us such crackpot names as Salop and did

away with Rutland. Happily, Rutland has returned and Shropshire regained its sensible name. Bebington is a mixture of two Bebingtons, Higher and Lower. In another life they were also called Superior and Nether. The 'ton' in the town name is Anglo Saxon for farm. The land was home to just a handful of sleepy, scattered hamlets until the Chester-Birkenhead stagecoach woke them up. The introduction of a steam ferry across the Mersey helped further growth. Both Bebingtons and Bromborough became UDCs, merging as Bebington and Bromborough UDC in 1921. Other villages came under that umbrella in 1933 and a name change was needed. To use the name of every town and village was too unwieldy. Argument was fast and furious but, after a close vote, the name of Bebington was the single one to go on the headed notepaper.

This aerial view of Birkenhead was captured on 15 February 1923. Aeroplane development had come a long way in the 20 years since Orville and Wilbur Wright showed that powered flight was possible at Kittyhawk. Major advances happened during World War I. It is always the same. It takes conflict to get things moving. To keep one step ahead of the enemy it was necessary to speed up development. Peacetime aviation got the benefit, but at what cost? During the war, planes were used as much on reconnaissance as they were in dogfights with Baron von Richtofen. Valuable information about fuel and ammunition depots, troop movements and defences were brought back on film from behind enemy lines. Perhaps the pilot taking this shot had gained his experience from flying one of those missions. He took a good photo. The camera has picked out many of Birkenhead's important features. Mighty ships were lined up in the docks next to Woodside, which can be seen at the bottom, to the right. In the left centre stands Birkenhead Town Hall, with Hamilton Square behind it where the memorial to Queen Victoria holds pride of place. It was in 1828 that the story of Birkenhead Dock began. However, it was not until 1843 that the general layout we can now see was established. The right hand side of the picture shows the source of the lifeblood of Birkenhead. These are some of the docks that helped its Victorian prosperity continue into the first half of the 20th century. Morpeth, Wallasey, Alfred and Vittoria are the names of some of the docks that seem to have been with us as long as we can remember.

At the launch of the 'Windsor Castle' 50,000 spectators lined the Mersey to watch her leave

There is nothing quite like the sight of a great ship to stir the blood, especially if it has such graceful lines as the 'Windsor Castle', seen here in 1960 with a posse of attendant tugs and pilots fussing around it. The construction of this ship by Cammell Laird was a prestige project, the biggest of its kind since the launch of the Cunard White Star liner, 'Mauretania', in 1938. The latter had been an unashamed luxury passenger liner, with a dance hall, cinemas, gyms, a swimming pool and a Turkish Bath. 'Windsor Castle' was built at Birkenhead between 1957 and 1959 for the Union Castle Mail Steamship Co, having the dual purpose of carrying mail on the South Africa route along with passengers in top-class accommodation. The completion of the ship was dogged by demarcation disputes in the Cammell Laird yards, but at her launch in 1959 the 38,000 ton 'Windsor Castle' was the largest of her kind ever to have been built at an English shipyard. The Queen Mother launched the ship, and it is proof of the attraction of such a spectacle that around 50,000 spectators found vantage points to watch the great liner slip away into the Mersey.

Left: This panoramic view of Hamilton Square was taken in 1921. Birkenhead was originally called Birchen Head, the headland of birch trees. Even 80 years ago, this was a densely built up area with nary a birch tree in sight. But the square provided a charming oasis of green in the centre of the town. The first Birkenhead Town Hall was built in 1835. In 1825 the building of Hamilton Square had begun and by 1839 the north side was completed. Between 1839-44 the south and west sides were built, leaving a gap for the town hall whose construction began in 1883. The Town Hall was damaged by fire in 1901 and restored by Henry Hartley. The design by CO Ellison & Son was chosen from 138. On 10 February 1887 a crowd of 5,000 watched the opening ceremony. Built from Shoreton stone and Scottish granite, it cost £43,000. The clock tower rises to 200 feet. The renovations cost £15,000. The gardens were purchased in 1903. The centre piece is a memorial to Queen Victoria, in the shape of an Eleanor Cross. The architect, Edmund Kirby, did not charge for his design. The 75 feet high octagonal memorial stands above Newby granite steps. The motto 'She brought her people lasting good' shows the affection that the nation had for Victoria. The cross takes its name from the memorials to Queen Eleanor, the beloved wife of Edward I, who died in Nottingham in 1290. Her funeral journey to Westminster was marked by a series of crosses placed at Grantham, Lincoln and the various other spots where her body rested en route to the capital.

Below: The best views of Wallasey Town Hall are from the air or over the rail of a ship making its way up the Mersey. It holds pride of place on Brighton Street, overlooking Seacombe Promenade. The building lies a good 70p bus ride from Wallasey Village and is a good example of the sort of muddled thinking and flawed reasoning you get from certain local politicians and worthies. In the early 20th century there was a great deal of discussion about the building that was to be the administrative face of Wallasey. To site it in the village under whose name the collection of small communities was gathered must have seemed too obvious. There was argument back and forth until a conclusion was reached. It was finally decided that Egremont and Seacombe provided the major gateways to the rest of the world, particularly via the ferries. Other links were completely ignored. With a lack of foresight, no account was taken of the effect that any future developments might have. So, Wallasey Town Hall ended up here. The foundation stone for the building was laid in 1914 George V gave it his royal blessing by performing the ceremony. The year was significant. Within a short time Archduke Franz Ferdinand, heir to the Hapsburg throne, had been assassinated and a world war was to break out. The Town Hall was requisitioned as a military hospital and did not become the Town Hall proper until November 1920. It is a beautiful building, but best seen from the river it faces. Entrance is made to it round the back!

Want to catch a bus? This is the site of the modern terminus, but it was a different scene in 1926. There were plenty of cars about and pedestrians took their lives in their hands as they dodged Morris Cowleys, Austin Wolseleys and Model T Fords on Woodside. Ferry boats used to leave from here at a rate of one every 20 minutes. The Woodside Hotel, at the top of the picture, is still a reminder of those frenetic days. Off to the right stood Shore Road Pumping Station. It is now the site of a business park. Britain had won the Great War, but it was struggling to win the peace. The government made bright promises after the war. Britain was to be a prosperous place, one of change for the better. The public and the returning heroes were optimistic. The mood was to change. Improvement in housing and working conditions failed to materialise. Worse still, miners had their wages cut. The slogan 'Not a penny off the pay, not a minute on the day' rang out across the land. People milling around Woodside were part of the general strike called by the TUC in support of the miners. Some 3,000,000 of the 5,000,000 members downed tools on 5 May. Daily Mail printers refused to print an editorial criticising the unions and the government declared a state of emergency. It became something of a class war. Middle class volunteers climbed on locomotive footplates, delivered the mail and drove buses to break the strike. Troops were brought in to keep other services going. The TUC backed off and left the miners to fight alone. Their dispute lasted for six months and left them bitter.

On the move

Above: The Leyland Titan PD/12 no 256 double decker bus was at the Arrowe Park roundabout in 1955. Motor buses had been running on the Wirral since 1919, when the first ran between Rock Ferry and Park Station. There are now shops behind the bus and beyond lies the Woodchurch estate. Pretty names like Meadow Crescent, Yew Tree Close and Greenwood Road suggest a spot of rural beauty. That was what the planners had hoped for. Sir Charles Reilly designed an estate that would have a village green, with small communities linked around it. His idea was thrown out in 1946. An alternative open layout was considered, with cottage style homes. That was abandoned in 1952.

In a rush to provide new housing to replace the town's old two up, two down terraced properties, along came high density housing and the inevitable tower blocks. Many who moved in regretted it. They missed the friendliness of their neighbours in the old back to backs. But, it was too late. The die was cast. The new Woodchurch residents were stuck in a drab environment. The little hamlet that had flowery tracks and grassy fields had disappeared under the unforgiving boot of progress. No more ploughing matches, shining horse brasses or picking blackberries for a tasty teatime pie; kiss them goodbye. The no 71 bus was on its way to Woodside. Perhaps the old Woodchurch residents were making a getaway before it was too late.

Above: Donkey rides at New Brighton were popular with the children. No visit was complete without an ice cream, a bucket and spade and a ride across the sands. But a ride on a camel? That was something else. This ship of the desert was not by the sea front to lead a caravan of kiddies across the sands. His was an advertising role. To try to grab public imagination and attention this gimmick was supposed to make you want to travel on one of Hardings' luxury coaches. They do not look too plush to our modern eyes, but in the early 1950s these were about as good as you got. Aboard a 'chara' families went off on day trips to Llandudno or Tenby. Trips to the gardens at Alton Towers, in the days before roller coasters and theme parks dominated such places, were always well supported. Then, in late September or October, came the almost compulsory visit to Blackpool Illuminations. On the way home we always called at a chippy for the customary cod and six pennyworth. Heavily salted, with vinegar running through the newspaper, they were a delicacy that southern softies with their horrible jellied eels could never appreciate. On the way home we sang 'How much is that doggy in the window?' and passed the hat round for the driver. He must have hated the smell of fish and chips by the end of the season.

Above right: This was certainly the shape of things to come in the bus world in 1960. A very new-looking front entry type model stands in all its splendour at the approach to Seacombe Ferry, whilst a line of older style buses is visible in the background. These sleek new arrivals usually heralded one-man operations and the disappearance of the conductor.

There had been plenty of changes in the ferry world too since that remarkable day, in 1817, when the steam paddle boat ferry, 'Etna', had appeared on the Mersey. Steamers were not at the mercy of wind and tide, and regular timetabled services across the river could begin. The ferries entered their golden years, but no one fully appreciated the devastating effect that the opening of the Queensway Tunnel in 1934 would have. Goods could now be carried by road beneath the Mersey and ferry revenues for goods traffic fell dramatically. The Seacombe luggage boats ceased to operate in 1947, after a war in which the ferries had often performed 'other duties'. The Kingsway Tunnel of 1971, between Wallasey and Liverpool, caused a further decline in ferry passenger traffic. Therefore, in 1989, the ferries were 'reinvented' as a visitor attraction in the shape of the highly successful Mersey Ferries Heritage Cruises, based at Seacombe.

Right: The weighing machine at the entrance to Crosville Bus Station used to show you your weight for just a single penny. Unfortunately, the finger on the big dial was so obvious that it let everybody else see. The bus has an advert for Vernons Pools that was to try to rival the bigger Littlewoods. Others had a go, particularly Zetters, but the Moores family enterprise reigned supreme. Even Premium Bonds, in the late 1950s, did not stop the Saturday night ritual of checking for eight draws and a big win. Then it was thousands. Now, the National Lottery has made it millions and pools companies struggle to compete. The bus station at Heswall was photographed in 1952. Heswall was where many merchant barons built summer homes . It was close enough to Birkenhead to be reached by horse and carriage. Those homes became their permanent residence as the roads and railways opened up commuter routes. Heswall was mentioned in the Domesday Book as Eswelle. It only grew in significance in the second half of the last century. The Crosville Motor Company developed from an electrical machinery firm set up by George Crosland Taylor (1857-1923) in 1882. He began assembling cars in 1906 and began a bus service from Ellesmere Port to Chester in 1911. During World War I his buses carried munitions workers to and from Mold. In 1928 Crosville buses sent tours to Devon and Scotland. By 1929 it was the third largest provincial bus company. It is now part of the National Bus Company.

Below: The lights of Hoylake Station glowed a welcome to travellers in 1952. It was a year when Jo Stafford and Al Martino were popular singers. England's very own Jimmy Young was a top crooner and Winston Churchill was in charge at 10 Downing Street. We were getting back on our feet after the war, though life was still not all roses. Rationing of some goods was still in place. Some sat on the train and grumbled about who had really won the war. There was trouble in Indo China and an atmosphere with Russia that old Winnie described as the pulling down of an iron curtain. In Hoylake it was peaceful. No one on the road, pedestrian or motorist. A century before, locals had to travel on foot or by bumpy horse drawn bus along the Woodside turnpike. That opened in 1841. Before then it had been an even more uncomfortably slow journey anywhere by pony and trap. A railway line to Birkenhead docks was laid in 1866. The joy of Hoylake residents at this event was short-lived. Financial problems led to the line's seizure by bailiffs in 1870. For two years the nearest station was at Bidston. Even after the Hoylake link was reopened there were grumblings about the high cost of travel. The line's reputation suffered a further setback in the 1880s when a serious crash occurred, just outside the station. The locomotive's stoker died in the accident. Public confidence was rocked for a time, but the convenience of rail travel soon won passengers back. Hoylake was one of the pretty places to where Liverpool merchants and businessmen had moved to live. Commuters to the city became regular passengers and the railway prospered.

D Morgan plc - pure land genius

In the first year of the new millennium fifty people were invited to an evening at Chomondley Castle in Cheshire to celebrate the fiftieth anniversary of one of the Wirral's most respected companies: D Morgan plc with its administrative base in Ellesmere Port.

It is known throughout Northern England & North Wales for its specialisation in urban regeneration including the remediation and re-use of derelict, and often contaminated land referred to by Local Authorities as 'brownfield land'. Central government policy seeks to recycle land. It does this by restricting planning permissions for new construction and new housing to 'brownfield' development land which has been cleared of its former uses. Recycling of land in this way avoids unnecessary expansion onto greenfield sites in open countryside. The firm has responded to government policy and to its customers needs with great success. It has a rental fleet of earthmoving equipment comprising over 100 units, each one with its own skilled operator with many units employed in recycling brownfield land, often for new housing developments. The focus on re-cycling land to re-use it for new development has shaped D. Morgan plc as we know it today, providing its customers with 'in-house' professional advice in response to legislation requiring a specialisation which the Company does offer.

Being at the right place at the right time and able to respond rapidly to commercial opportunities as they arise is still the main reason why any business remains successful. The equipment used by the Company can often cost between £50,000 to £300,000 per unit. The firm owns over 100 such units. It employs 240 people. With this large 'in-house' resource it can respond rapidly to any customers needs.

It is a legacy of Britain's industrial heritage as a trading nation, developing world trade in the nineteenth century that has left the British Isles with many sites occupied by former redundant industrial uses. Such land must now be re-used. It is only now that many of the 'original' nineteenth century industrial sites often in our inner cities are being re-cycled and re-developed usually for housing.

D Morgan plc has been involved in many projects. It has the capability and experience to help its customers cope with these new challenges.

In the year 2000 not only is this company celebrating fifty years in business it is also a remarkable opportunity to celebrate Mrs Ursula Morgan's fifty years with the firm. She had set out in 1950 supporting her husband in building up the company from nothing, using their fifty pounds savings with which they purchased their first vehicle. Mrs Morgan took charge of the administration whilst her husband Denis found work and developed relationships with the company's first customers.

The late Mr Denis Morgan, originally from Rhosmedre near Llangollen North Wales, served his country as Sergeant during the second world war in the Staffordshire and Somerset Light Infantry. Whilst serving in Germany Mr Morgan met his future wife, Ursula, and on his leaving the army in 1948 they married in Ellesmere Port. It was here that Denis was to find future work in the post war reconstruction of the UK economy with employment in Ellesmere port rapidly creating some 10,000 manufacturing jobs in new industries.

Denis Morgan's ambition had been to go into the road haulage business. He wanted to own his own lorry. In 1950 that ambition materialised when he acquired his first ex-

Above: *Mr and Mrs Denis Morgan on their wedding day in 1948. The firm was founded two years later in 1950.*

remember as a location for the Cheshire Agricultural Show in the early 1960s.

Needless to say a mechanical loading shovel was an important next purchase when sufficient money had been saved. There was no hire purchase agreement or small business start up bank loan back then. Many people as young as 30 years of age in the 1950s had experienced the worldwide depression and slump of the 1930s, followed by rationing throughout the war years of the 1940s. A general fear of incurring debt prevailed amongst this generation with a culture of saving money before most people purchased anything and did so only if they could afford it from their savings. The early years for all of these reasons were hard with long 12 hour days and a minimum six day week. Today the firm maintains two working vintage vehicles from that period kept as a reminder of how it all began. They can usually be seen on display at the major vintage rallies in Cheshire including the Chelford & Malpas transport rallies and at the Cheshire Agricultural Show.

military truck which was converted from a canvas backed troop-carrier into a tipper truck to haul sand. The road transport industry was at that time nationalised. Denis could not start trading until an operator's licence was issued by the relevant government agency. There were already several small haulage companies in the area, all of which objected to the award of any more licences. With perseverance Denis overcame these objections and eventually received the appropriate licence to operate his one truck.

There was plenty of construction work to do within the borough. In 1950 the construction of British Nuclear Fuels Factory in Capenhurst, E. Port was underway and also major expansion projects at the Shell oil refinery Stanlow, E. Port soon to become the second largest oil refinery in Europe.

A second truck had to be purchased to meet customer demand. Around that time Mr Morgan also received his first regular contract to supply sand to Hooton Aerodrome for the construction of a new runway there. It was hard work: the sand was hand loaded by Denis into the lorry from the sandpit at Pooltown Road Whitby, E. Port. Since that time Vauxhall Motors acquired the airfield and has its manufacturing plant located on the former airfield which many people will

It wasn't long before the long hours paid off and Denis Morgan managed to secure another regular contract. Contracting in a very small way was a major factor in the company's early growth providing some stability and continuity. The Company advertised itself in the 1950s as D Morgan Contractor. Bowater Paper Mill, Ellesmere Port located next to Vauxhall Motor's car plant needed to have woodbark regularly removed from its factory. The woodbark, stripped from trees prior to the timber being pulped to make paper was considered unsuitable for any use. How times have changed; today woodbark is used in gardens everywhere as mulch to reduce the growth of weeds. In the 1950s factories were prepared to pay contractors to dispose of it as a waste bi-product and Denis Morgan did so for many years.

After the first 10 years trading there was a need for the business to operate from its own premises rather than from Mr & Mrs Morgan's home. In 1964 the business relocated

Above: Mr Morgan in the 1950s.
Below: A low loader to carry machinery in the 1960s.

within the borough of Ellesmere Port to Great Sutton, where a one acre farm building complex, including farm house, was purchased for £6,500. It was the first bank loan taken on by the Company. It was a major decision to invest in the Company's longer term future to grow the business. Redundant farm buildings were converted to workshops and offices with sufficient vehicle parking remaining available within the farmyard. Ursula Morgan continued to support her husband in growing the business as she would do for many more decades to come. The Company eventually outgrew these premises.

In 1981 Hooton Brickworks comprising a factory recently closed standing in 45 acres of land (19 hectares) was purchased for £330,000 and all the workshops and parking of vehicles/equipment was gradually transferred from Great Sutton to the much larger Hooton premises today known as Hooton Logistics Park. The Great Sutton former farm buildings were demolished and the Great Sutton site re-developed, with new buildings becoming the administrative centre.

Technology has always played its part in creating greater efficiencies and in 1960 the widespread introduction of the first hydraulic excavators resulted in the Company purchasing a now very familiar JCB excavator. Hydraulically operated machinery was a new concept: previously it was mechanically operated by wire ropes and pulleys with winches. Denis Morgan purchased his first JCB to hire out to local builders. This purchase saw the expansion of the company throughout the 1960s, becoming the largest local Company hiring out modern hydraulic equipment which could carry out tasks previously requiring manual labour. The hire of equipment into the construction industry and to house builders continues to this day.

During the early years business was mostly local, within the borough of Ellesmere Port, due in part to the restrictive road network. Remember this was before the now familiar Runcorn Bridge over the River Mersey was opened by

Princess Alexandra of Kent in 1961. It is perhaps unbelievable that what you see as the present Runcorn bridge replaced a 'transporter' lift suspended on a gantry across the River Mersey. The lift was winched across the gantry by cables restricting the crossing to the combined weight of just a few vehicles in what effectively was a large cable car carrying vehicles across the River. A regularly undertaken journey during this period before Motorways were built was to Leeds for equipment parts. This took a mechanic on a good day at least 10 hours round trip in the company Mini; a return journey now possible in under three hours.

In the 1970s the expanding motorway network opened up the whole north-west region to the Company. In a one hour journey the firm's vehicles would in previous years have travelled through towns and city centres covering distances of just fifteen miles; now in that same hour a vehicle could be fifty miles away on a motorway.

The years 1972-74 saw other changes with the introduction of new pollution control legislation. It was then that central government took a serious interest in the environment with an extra tier of statutory controls through the issue of waste disposal licences to companies wishing to carry out a waste disposal service. These licences could be withdrawn if a company offended against statutory controls. Many of the Company's customers not wishing themselves to obtain waste disposal licences in disposing of their waste products wanted to buy in this service and the new legislation led to the creation of a separate management team, which in due course developed activities in waste recycling. More environmental legislation followed, requiring greater specialisation which has attracted a growing customer base which the Company responded to by expanding through the intervening years into becoming the UK's largest specialist in the field of urban reclamation and recycling of contaminated land within the geographical areas of the West Midlands, Pennine region, Greater Manchester, North West England and North Wales

Above: *Mr and Mrs Morgan in the 1950s.*

and in recent years North, South & West Yorkshire. The firm takes on contracts valued from less than £10,000 up to the largest single contract to date of £4.8 million.

Throughout its existence resource management to provide customer services also meant cash management. Mrs Morgan set resolute standards in the early years with the Company never borrowing beyond its means. A cautious view and the reluctance to fund growth by taking on too much borrowed money has proved to be the right approach on several occasions. In the early 70s UK property prices slumped, which almost saw the closure of the National Westminster Bank, only prevented by the Bank of England setting up a 'lifeboat' fund, providing much needed extra cash to shore up the exposed banking sector including the NatWest Bank's balance sheet which at that time was insolvent. The UK property and banking crisis of the 1970s and NatWest's own cash problems almost stopped Morgan's steady growth in the 1970s and eventually led to a change of banks to Barclays. The change in banks was a decision taken in 1980 because Barclays understood and was prepared to support the firm's business development goals over the next 10 years. It was the first major decision taken by Denis Morgan jnr in establishing the Company's future direction.

In the 198□s the firm expanded into other areas including brickmaking

Sadly in 1978, Mr Denis Morgan, the firm's founder, died after a long illness. Denis Morgan jnr, the founder's son, however had joined the firm in 1974 at the age of 22; that same year Barbara Bates nee Morgan also began working for the firm after working for a Local Authority as a librarian, and in 1980 a third member Karin Wildman nee Morgan also joined the family team after working as the personal secretary for the Borough Engineer of Ellesmere Port Council. Lorraine Dennan nee Morgan worked for Shell and whilst not joining the business her husband John Dennan decided to leave his employment with Manweb and did join in 1977.

The years from 1980 onwards saw the firm expanding. By 1980 the Company needed to strengthen its management team and Company Secretary Mrs Margaret Barker took up her post which she still controls today. In 1982 Mr Alan Burns joined the Company as a Director with John Dennan appointed a Director in 1991. Both Directors remain with the Company. The responsibility upon Mrs Ursula Morgan and Denis Morgan jnr was in this way shared between a greater number of senior people. The firm continued expanding but

Below: *Ronnie Walters, the firm's third employee, who retired in 1999, in a picture dating from the 1960s.*

the next move was not predictable by anyone outside of the boardroom. It changed direction and purchased brick manufacturing premises. Brickworks eventually owned by Morgan's include: Hooton Brickworks Wirral, now a warehouse and distribution depot; Moreton-Carr Lane Brickworks Wirral; which was the last brickworks to be operated by the firm making up to 230,000 bricks per week up until 1991; New Hey Brickworks in Rochdale, Alltami at Mold North Wales; and Bold Heath St Helens, now a large quarry. It also acquired several other mineral extraction locations. The quarrying and brick manufacturing businesses purchased throughout the 1980s meant that the land surrounding the firm's quarries is now either farmed, tenanted or let annually to local people. Over 700 acres were acquired during this period enabling the firm to secure its long term future set out by Denis Morgan jnr in the late 1970s.

Although the firm no longer makes bricks, the raw material, clay and shale, is still quarried. Morgan's continue to supply quarried materials into the construction industry and brick manufacturing industry, using its fleet of over 60 trucks. The technical, geological, environmental and other statutory requirements and controls associated with mineral extraction are not dissimilar to the understanding of waste disposal requirements, how to ensure for example that landfill sites, typically in worked-out quarries are infilled with waste materials and finally restored and returned to agricultural land or to woodland.

A recurring theme of the Morgan business is that each part is in some way interconnected, each part linking with other activities and each component contributing to the greater strength of the whole, although there have been closures along the way in activities where the business did not have a strong record of success and lost money.
The lesson of being very good at what you do for your customers and if possible better than your competitors has long been learned. If you can't achieve this then you will

always be second best and struggle to survive in a very competitive world.

As might be expected the cyclical economic climate (the boom and bust economic cycle) produced more ups and downs for the firm with the early 1980s producing another difficult recession for the British economy, this time caused by a Middle East oil crisis which for those who are old enough to remember did result in UK fuel rationing by our government to ease the fuel shortage. It was a concern at that time that not only was the cost of fuel escalating whether you could obtain any fuel supplies at all to run your business was a bigger issue.

Ever resourceful and innovative, by 1984 the worst of the Middle East oil crisis was over and trading conditions became very favourable with the Company generally expanding 'on all fronts' until 1989, when the country was plunged into a sudden deep recession. This time it was caused by ever increasing inflation which brought with it an investment surge (benefiting from inflation) with everyone happy until it came to an abrupt end. By this time and after five good years' earnings growth many people had been encouraged to spend their money in buying their own houses and the infamous negative equity trap caused by the 1989 sudden recession and drop in values meant that there was a huge amount of personal debt left owing to many banks with the value of people's houses having fallen steeply.

Bank loans were called in, houses were repossessed throughout the country. It was during the early 1990s that the Company's largest ever bad debts amounting to £450,000 were incurred in one year as many banks called in company overdrafts and appointed receivers to longstanding customers in an attempt to recover unpaid loans. The bad debts were

Above: *The farm purchased for £6,500 in 1964, now demolished and redeveloped as the Company's administrative base.*

overcome because D Morgan's own balance sheet remained very strong, due to the Company's reluctance to borrow too much money to fund its growth, preferring instead to remain cautious which time and again has proved to be the right policy, as others have failed with too much debt to repay when recessions occur. Although it is not immune from the effects of periodic recessions, the firm has always been strong enough to trade through each downturn, coping well with the problems. Fortunately such setbacks and problems which drove so many others out of business acted as a spur to greater efforts and the business emerged stronger and more focused than ever consolidating its position through the early 1990s. In 1997 the business banked its first seven figure cheque for one million and forty four thousand pounds, representing the most concentrated period of high value work, for just one of its many customers, carried out in only six weeks, demonstrating just how capable the firm had become in resourcing its customers' particular needs.

The firm's civil engineering department during the 1990s has also come to specialise, for example in water based projects including Liverpool Marina and coastal works in strengthening sea defences. Refurbishment and building of bridges often needed to cross water have become an extension of this water related specialisation including canal restoration schemes for British Waterways.

As part of the Y2K celebrations a government funded Millennium bridge in St Helens was recently constructed by the Company using new technology developed jointly with design consultants Ove Arup & Partners and architects Cass Associates in consultation with the University of Manchester Institute of Science & Technology (UMIST). Applications for use of this new technology and enquiries from consultants are coming in from other parts of the world with the company currently involved in the design for a project in the Middle East. Whilst the company will not itself work outside the UK it will assist in the transfer of this technology.

The company's engineering knowledge of bridges and of other complex structures enables the firm to demolish such structures, producing its own method statements, identifying the correct sequence of working to ensure that even the most difficult demolition and dismantling work complies with Health and Safety legislation causing the least disruption to a client's site. The firm offers a range of solutions in its ability to carry out dismantling of potentially dangerous vessels and structures. Methods used include temporary propping, remote working, hydrodemolition and controlled cold cutting. Such methods used in conjunction with specially

Below: *One of the early JCB hydraulic excavators, purchased in 1967.*

modified hydraulic excavators have even enabled the firm to demolish steel and concrete vessels containing explosive and toxic liquids without risk of injury or damage to the environment.

Risk Assessment is now a crucial element in any preparation, whether digging a trench with a JCB in the presence of underground electricity or telecommunication cables supplying our towns and cities or in identifying and then isolating hazards and in the use of safe working procedures.

By the end of the century Mr Denis Morgan jnr celebrated 26 years working in the business, concurrent with Mrs Ursula Morgan's 50 years in the business. The current chairman has responsibility for policy decisions involving 240 employees covering a range of activities from road management (building to maintaining) and operating the largest tipper vehicle fleet for hire and use in the North of England. It also has available a large earth moving plant fleet and the firm enjoys a reputation for undertaking 'fast track' civil engineering projects especially involving water based projects and bridge construction or dismantling.

The firm's reputation has continued to develop in the last five years from its involvement in projects for Manchester & Liverpool airports where hi-specification work and safety procedures are paramount in completing work ahead of

schedule. This expertise has broadened the customer base to include Government Agencies including the Department of Environment, Transport & Regions (DETR) with many highway contracts requiring complicated traffic management schemes with roads kept open to traffic as road improvement schemes are carried out avoiding total closure.

Today the company, still family owned, is a highly respected and financially secure Group with 50 years experience. It has major financial investments and expertise enabling it to fund and offer clients warranties on large 'brownfield' land developments in re-cycling land for new uses and is able to purchase expensive heavy earthmoving equipment costing between £50,000 and £300,000 per unit with land assets including quarries, waste recycling, landfilling facilities. It also not surprisingly keeps available significant cash resources to reduce its dependency on debt finance when 'recessions' periodically occur, usually it is noted from past experience during the first few years at the start of each new decade.

The firm has developed its corporate structure keeping people as its main asset and for this reason the size of the business is often thought to be smaller than it is because its personal

Above: *A34 Wilmslow Bypass - installation of railway bridge in the mid 1990s. 5,000 tonnes of earth were moved by the company in five hours.*

assessment driven by the need to improve and develop new skills to implement modern methods, using all the latest available technology needed to continually move the business forward and move the customers business forward.

Morgan's have adapted to the challenges and opportunities presented to it over the years learning from both its many successes and some failures. It has always been managed as a business strong on relationship building. Because of its performance over many years the business has received more work from its customers, both locally based and regionally based with international blue chip organisations and government agencies now also relying on the business to provide a regional service to them. 'Partnering' is a word much used to forge a stronger bond and relationship with customers. It is however what the past 50 years have all been about in D Morgan plc in the family business partnering its employees and in its employees partnering its customers.

attitudes unique to a family business have changed little over the years with its people still being the most important part of the business with whom customer contact is focused. To achieve this close co-operation between people the business is managed in small teams each specialising in one function or area of expertise. Personal relationships remain important in this business. Without the right people no organisation can succeed in performing all of the many different tasks its customers require. All employees for over two decades have been involved in training programmes with an annual

*Above: Gerald Gould (Senior Partner of the firm's auditors), Mrs Ursula Morgan and Barry Marsh (Senior Partner of the firm's solicitors) in a picture dating from 1989. **Right:** Mrs Janina and Mr Denis Morgan (the current Chairman). **Below:** A 35 tonne excavator from a fleet of 100 units loading up one of the fleet of sixty-eight wheel tipper wagons.*

To grow from a family business with a single lorry in 1950, from a mere fifty pounds investment into a family business operating on this scale is remarkable. It is an extraordinary tribute to the hard work and commitment of Denis Morgan snr and his wife Ursula in creating a future for themselves, and for their family in the post war years and in so doing creating an organisation capable of providing a future for 240 people working in it today.

Ellesmere Port Collection

Down by the waterside

The dockside at Ellesmere Port was pictured at one of its many busy times. The hustle and bustle along the waterfront was vital to the economy of the Wirral. The large cranes used to hoist goods high into the air have disappeared, as has the sugar cane factory that stood at the far end. Even so, it is still a vibrant part of the peninsula. Timber and automobiles are moved on from here, while, further along, the tankers at the Shell and Burmah refineries stand in line. The port grew out of Whitby Locks, as the locks on the canal basin were known. Eventually, common usage saw the name become the Port of Ellesmere, before settling on Ellesmere Port as the title in the early 19th century.

The importance of the dock can be seen from the way that the first housing grew up around it. The first main street was called Dock Street. Trade developed along the Shropshire Union Canal. But, it was the coming of the Manchester Ship Canal that led to the real growth of the docks in the early years of the last century. By 1950 there were 1,641 acres in industrial use. Although there was a dip in fortunes after the middle of the 20th century, there was another boom in later years. The large development of the Stanlow Shell plant helped revitalise the area. By 1970 it had an investment there of £150 million. The refinery at Eastham added to the wealth and the bright future around Ellesmere Port.

Below: Did these lads ever get to work in the docks? By now they will be in their fifties. How did life treat them in the second half of the 20th century as they grew up? They were part of the postwar baby boom that began when servicemen came home from overseas. Many had been away for years, fighting on foreign shores or locked away in prison camps. Back home they let nature take its course and the sales of maternity frocks and Silver Cross prams rocketed. It was also a time when other men came back to find that wives and sweethearts had not waited. They had forged other relationships and the divorce courts became another growth industry. In 1958, when this group was looking at Woodside's new graving dock, Britain and its shipping was back on an even keel. As the concrete piles were being driven into the dock, the postwar economy was just as firm and secure. We were approaching the 'never had it so good' days. Unemployment was low and consumers were able to spend freely. The boys would come to manhood in the swinging '60s and be in early middle age when the new millennium dawned. Are they still in Birkenhead? In years to come, will they take their grandchildren down to Woodside and tell them of the fall in fortunes that came, only to be followed by a regeneration that pleased us all?

Bottom: As an island race it is only right that we should be good on water. Messing about in boats is a favourite pastime. For some it means sailing little dinghies on lakes and for others slaloming along a river in a kayak. Then, there is team rowing. The Henley Regatta is the most famous of our rowing festivals and the annual Boat Race between Oxford and Cambridge the best known single event. In the Olympic Games we have had more success on water than in most other sports. Stephen Redgrave, our best ever oarsman, has a host of gold medals, dating back to the first one he won in

1984. He did not pick up his armful of awards without a lot of hard work. Pulling an oar is very demanding. To do it in co-operation with a group of others demands practice and togetherness. In March 1938, listening to the coach bellowing instructions through his megaphone, a coxed four was being put through its paces for a special event on 2 April 1938. The team was training in the Great Float at Birkenhead in readiness for the Shrewsbury head of the river race. It was to be a test of their skill, for the crew had never rowed in such an important event before. Wallasey Grammar School rowing team had won many prizes in more local events, but this was the big one. If it won, then the cox was in for a ducking as it was the traditional way for a crew to celebrate. He could not object. He was half the size of an oarsman!

The Woodside ferry building and bus station is given an impressive backdrop in this 1954 shot. Across the Mersey the dazzling white liner, 'Reina del Pacifico', immediately catches the eye. Standing behind the liner are buildings which may well be an unremarkable sight to Birkonians, but are impressive nonetheless - that famous waterfront image of the Royal Liver Building, the Cunard Steamship Company Building and the copper dome of the Mersey Docks and Harbour Company. The transport on view at Woodside bus station in 1954 certainly looks historical to the modern eye, and in other respects this area has some

interesting links with the past. In 1898 the Owen family moved from Oswestry in Shropshire to Birkenhead, and whilst Mr Owen did his duties at Woodside Railway Station, his son, Wilfred, attended the Birkenhead Institute. Wilfred Owen became one of the most famous of the war poets, tragically losing his life in 1918, in the very last stages of World War I. Woodside, of course, is mainly associated with the famous Mersey ferries, which have plied their trade from at least the fourteenth century. They now form part of the local heritage industry, with cruises beginning at Woodside, whilst the old booking hall serves as a visitor centre.

Above: The sheer massive scale of shipbuilding is illustrated by this 1948 picture of one of the Cammell Laird yards. Painting is in progress, both at ground level and from tall stepladders, but the men seem dwarfed by the towering ship. Even the links of the chains are huge - as if forged by giants. The history of shipbuilding at Cammell Laird has been full of superlatives relating to size. In 1912 the largest floating dock in the world was built at Birkenhead. When the 'Windsor Castle' was launched in 1959 it was the largest ship of her kind ever to have been built in an English shipyard. Even in the 'twilight' years, when Cammell Laird had become part of British Shipbuilders, a huge construction hall was built in 1978 for indoor shipbuilding, costing £32 million, one that dominated the Birkenhead waterfront. At the time of the photograph, 1948, Britain had just emerged from a devastating war, and once again some impressive statistics are on record. Between 1939 and 1945 Cammell Laird built 106 fighting ships, an average of one every twenty days in spite of the attentions of the Luftwaffe. During this war 75 million tonnes of cargo and 4.7 million troops passed through Liverpool.

Above: The ship standing at Birkenhead docks was the Clan Farquharson. The docks that had seen such famous ships such as Achilles (1931), Ark Royal (1937), Prince of Wales (1939) and Thetis (1939) sail out of the Cammell Laird shipyards, was still a busy place in the 1950s. It could trace its roots back to the rapid development that began with the establishment of boiler works and a shipyard on Wallasey Pool. That was established in 1824 by William Laird, a pioneer in the construction of iron ships. Laird also laid out the nucleus of the town on a grid plan. Laird's combined with Cammell's shipbuilding company in 1903. By the 1970s, the dockland was a sadder place as shipping declined. The revival in Birkenhead's fortunes in recent times was a blessing. Alfred Dock and the entrances to the northern dock system were opened in 1866. Lights have replaced bobbies on point duty at the Duke Street entrance to Vittoria Dock. There was something homely about the British bobby on point duty. His was an awesome power. With one sweeping motion of a white gloved arm, he could release a fleet of lorries along the road. When a palm was thrust aloft everything ground to a halt. Not for our man the whistles and histrionic flapping of the continental gendarme. Britons carried out their job calmly and with dignity.

Above right: A sad sight indeed as the passenger liner, 'Empress of Canada', lies on her side in Gladstone Dock, totally gutted by a devastating fire in January 1953. The 'Empress of Canada' was a ship that was well-known in more than one guise to those who lived along the banks of the Mersey. In her first manifestation she was the pre-war Canadian Pacific liner, 'Duchess of Richmond', and like so many ships of her type she adopted a new role for the duration of World War II. In the main this was troop carrying, and the 'Duchess' made trips to Suez, India, North Africa and the Mediterranean. She also made a trip to Odessa, on the Black Sea, carrying released Russian prisoners of war, in 1945. After the war the ship was reconditioned as a first-class passenger liner on the Liverpool to Canada run, and renamed 'Empress of Canada'. The disastrous fire at Gladstone Dock came immediately after an overhaul in January 1953. Nothing could be done to control the blaze, and the amount of water shipped caused the vessel to keel over onto its side. The raising of the ship in 1954 was a huge job, involving buoyancy pontoons and massive steam winches and hawsers. The hulk was then sold as scrap.

This page: The cameraman on this occasion *(bottom)* has chosen not to concentrate on the action, but the reponses to the action. Hence the photograph of a well-dressed crowd seemingly cheering and waving at nothing. In a more elevated if precarious position, some workers are also enjoying the occasion. And the cause of all the excitement? The second photograph *(right)* gives the answer - a ship glides down the slipway at its launching. This is always an impressive event, even a moving one as an inanimate object somehow seems to take on a life of its own. For the watching workers it can be a moment of great pride, a culmination of perhaps years of collective effort. The launching in question was that of the 'Cheshire', on April 23rd 1959. Its keel had been laid on July 22nd 1958 at the Cammell Laird shipyards. A cargo ship of 7,201 tons, the 'Cheshire' was built on behalf of Bibby Bros, a local firm, and in fact Lady Bibby performed the honours at the launching. Beneath the glamour and excitement of it all ran a slight thread of pessimism, for cargo ships are built from a commercial point of view, in the hope of making a profit, and in the late 1950s it was clear that there was over-capacity in the world's merchant fleets.

Competition for trade was intense and freight rates low. Within this scenario the launching of the 'Cheshire' was an act of faith, and at the post-launch luncheon the Chairman of Bibby Bros, Major Sir A Harold Bibby, cast doubts as to whether the ship would ever make a profit in existing conditions. Fortunately the Cammell Laird shipyards did not rely entirely on building general purpose cargo ships, and some of the contracts the company worked on in the 1950s and 1960s showed the diversity of its output. Government orders were especially valuable, from the building of the second 'Ark Royal' aircraft carrier in 1955 through to the commissioning of two nuclear powered Polaris Submarines in 1963. The trend towards ever larger oil tankers was a profitable one for Cammell Laird, with the 65,500 ton tanker 'Sepia' being launched in 1961. In this respect, a £17 million scheme resulted in the opening of the new Princess Dock in 1962, a large dry dock for building bigger tankers. However, perhaps Major Bibby's gloom was partly induced by the labour troubles that had dogged the construction of the prestige ship 'Windsor Castle', launched in 1959, the same year as the 'Cheshire'.

A vintage picture of the 'roaring 20s' finds the approach to Seacombe Ferry packed with cars and people. Surely some great event is in prospect, for everyone is dressed in their best, with a touch of fur here and there, and those fine ladies' cloche hats well in evidence. The cars too are a delight to behold, although they probably gave a rough ride by modern standards, especially on all those cobbled surfaces. The start of an organised ferry service across the Mersey came in 1330, when the monks of 'Birchen Head' Priory were given the exclusive right by

Edward II to ferry travellers from the point which became known as Monk's Ferry. A separate privilege was granted to the Earl Of Chester to run a ferry from 'Seccum' (Seacombe) to Birkenhead. After Birkenhead Priory was 'dissolved' by Henry VIII, in 1536, the ferry rights tended to be held by wealthy families for some years, but the tides and cross-winds always held the possibility of danger and delay for sail boats. It was the advent of steam power in 1817 that produced safe and regular services, regardless of the weather, and by the 1920s the Seacombe Ferry was carrying nearly 32 million passengers per year.

Bottom: Even in the 1940s, when this dramatic photograph was taken, the sea lashing across the promenade at Parkgate was an unusual sight. Now it would be a rarity indeed. In the eighteenth century, however, the deep-water anchorage at Parkgate made it the principal terminal for mail packets plying between England and Dublin. Many famous figures of that century passed through Parkgate including Handel, Swift and John Wesley. Not only this, the mud of this fashionable holiday resort was supposed to have curative properties for skin complaints, a claim that was put to the test by Lady Hamilton, Nelson's mistress. Gradually, however, the silting up which was affecting the whole of the Dee Estuary took its toll, and by 1810 the service to Dublin was virtually at an end. Parkgate was not quite left 'high and dry', for shrimp fishing continued to flourish. However, by the 1930s the sea was just about reaching the sea wall at high tide, and since then the view has increasingly been one of miles of salt marsh towards Wales, with little evidence of the sea. Nevertheless Parkgate has a fine frontage along the Parade, and older readers may well have happy memories of the Boathouse Tea Rooms. Visitors still enjoy the town's shrimps and ice-cream.

Right: Some of these lads must have been chilled to the bone in 1 March 1938. Their boots shone brightly on the soccer field as they were put through their paces. Practising their semaphore techniques, they were outside the Lancashire and National Sea Training Home at Wallasey. The centre was founded in 1901 by a group of ship owners. It was intended to be a form of nursery for Britain's young seamen. During the 1920s and 1930s there had been a revival in shipping. The Royal Navy had expanded rapidly. Demand

exceeded supply. There were not enough new recruits coming through to meet the shortfall. Great efforts were made by those on Merseyside to address the problem. Across the Channel, Germany was mobilising. Italy had been at war with Abyssinia and Spain was in the throes of a civil war. It was obvious to most people that the country needed to be on red alert for another war. The exception to that belief was our prime minister, Neville Chamberlain, who believed in the silly piece of paper he brought back from Munich. More and more young lads were trained. At any one time the centre held 150 on the training course that lasted for 18 to 24 months. When manpower runs short in times of war, it is younger and younger lads who are thrown into the fray. Before the second world war finished some of these youngsters would have become seafaring warriors before they were hardly old enough to shave.

Liverpool Libraries & Information Services

Ellesmere Port Collection

Shopping spree

Ellesmere Port - Whitby Road. Shopping here in 1961 was a busy and bustling experience. The cyclist and lorry are heading towards the station, away from the main shopping area. The car is turning onto the main street from Cromwell Road. Ellesmere Port gained borough status in 1955 as it had become such an important and thriving community. Although the businesses might have changed, the shops that can be seen are still there. There are now other ones on the opposite side of the road, as well. Tolls was the main department store, selling a variety of goods and clothing. Typical of many of its era, it was well patronised, but suffered from competition in later years when shoppers became more mobile. Instead of supporting their local store, they jumped into cars and went off into the larger establishments and big chain stores in Birkenhead, Chester and Liverpool. Tolls followed the same pattern as its fellows and had to close down. It became the Cycle and Pram Exchange. When that enterprise was closed after fire damaged the building in the late 1980s, it lay boarded up and unoccupied for years. So called artistic graffiti adorned its Cromwell Road side. The Queens, on the left, had been a cinema for 50 years at the time of this photograph. The main attraction on 16 February 1961 was 'Hannibal', starring Victor Mature. He was an actor of limited ability, but his darkly handsome looks and muscular physique made him ideal for epic roles in which he could take off his shirt and give smouldering looks.

Ellesmere Port Collection

Ellesmere Port - Whitby Road. The woman window shopping on the right must have felt uncomfortable without something with which she could cover her head. The headscarf helped her to feel ladylike. Her mother had always told her that only common folk go out without a hat on or smoke cigarettes in the street. Ellesmere Port's main street, Whitby Road, was packed with shoppers on this day. It must have been a Saturday to get so many out and about at the same time. The awnings had been pulled down to deflect any damage that the sun might do. The first thing the shopkeepers had done that morning was to get out their poles and pull down those multi purpose covers. As well as

being a defence against the sun, they protected shoppers from the rain and advertised the shop's business. Quite often, the awnings were used to trumpet the owner's name and the main lines he stocked. Some could look jolly with their candy stripes and bright colours. Halfway along Whitby Road, on the right, there is a Guinness advert. This company has become famous for its witty promotions. It was one of the first to recognise the power of humour. So, we had the crocodile and the toucan appearing on billboards. We read the slogan 'Guinness is good for you' and remembered it because of the antics and sayings of the creatures. Later television adverts used the same amusing approach.

Below: Birkenhead - Grange Road. The Morris Minor has become a collector's item. It is one of the best loved memories from the 1950s. The only way we can collect our memories of the store on the left is from photographs and our own recollections. This part of Grange Road is now a pedestrianised area. Half a century ago cars brought shoppers to Robb's department store. It was not just any shop. Entering Robb's was an experience with which few other establishments could compete. The tone was set as you approached the doors. An elegant doorman, resplendent in his top hat, greeted you politely and ushered you in. That was only the beginning of a visit to a world of charm, quality and sheer luxury. A beautifully ornate staircase took customers to the upper level. Descending it again made you think of debutantes sweeping down the steps as they entered a ballroom. Not everyone came to buy. Some just came along to enjoy the atmosphere and admire the goods that were on offer. It was chic and fashionable to shop at Robb's. People wanting to impress at a dinner party would answer a question about a purchase with a casual, 'Oh, just something I got from Robb's.' They were either impressed or thought you a real snob! As convenience and not quality became the catchword, Robb's went into decline. Its whole frontage is now filled by a number of smaller, separate outlets. Plush and style are no longer buzzwords.

Bottom: Liscard - Liscard Road. The name apparently means 'the fort on the height', which hints at some preoccupation with military matters amongst local people at some point deep in the past. However, the pedestrians featured in this 1965 shot of Liscard Road probably had more peaceful matters on their mind, no doubt relating to shopping. Liscard

in fact was a main shopping centre for this part of the Wirral in the nineteenth century. It was highly fashionable and patronised by ladies arriving in carriages and attended by servants. Speaking of fashion, a good array of 1960s styles is on view in the window of the Co-op, the store which dominates the photograph. It is difficult now to imagine what a central role was played by the Co-op in many people's lives for a good part of the twentieth century. It operated almost like a mini Welfare State, offering services from the 'cradle to the grave'. Your first baby clothes might be bought at the Co-op, and you might be finally laid to rest by its funeral services. In between the two events the Co-op could provide for almost everything. Part of the money you spent came back in the shape of the annual dividend, and some older people can instantly remember their old 'divi' number.

A Phoenix amongst markets

Long before out of town superstores, long before shopping malls - indeed long before shops as we know them today - came the market. Markets and market places have a unique place in the history of our towns and cities. Few towns do not have a Market Street or Market Place at their hub. The need to collect together those with goods to sell in one place at a predetermined time goes back beyond recorded history. At first markets were a come as you please venue, unregulated and disorganised with farmers, potters ironmongers and silversmiths mingling with weavers, butchers and candlestick makers each setting up stalls from scratch and competing with one another to get to the market place as early as possible in order to occupy the best pitch.

The most attractive feature of a market from a trader's point of view were the low operating costs. Unlike owning a shop, setting up a stall in a field requires no capital investment in bricks and mortar - although it does have the disadvantage that all the stock must be removed at the end of the day and carted off to the next market place. For the customer a market's low overheads meant that the

Below: *The market in the late 1950s.*

stall-holders' savings can be passed on to them in the form of lower prices.

The down side of an open market however has always been the fact that it is open to the elements - a particular disadvantage in Britain where the weather is to say the least unpredictable.

In the early 19th century a fashion began to provide covered accommodation for what had previously been open air markets. The idea caught on very quickly in a manner not dissimilar to the speed with which shopping centres sprang up in the late twentieth century. The variable British weather was one motive; others no doubt included the Victorian obsession with hygiene - and, perhaps more sinister, a desire on the part of the authorities to regulate and control the previously uncontrolled

and unregulated - a desire still in evidence today with the ongoing battle between those who would prefer to buy their spuds weighed in pounds and ounces and cloth measured in feet and inches rather than kilograms and grams or metres and centimetres.

The motives to build had existed since time immemorial, it was however the means that were lacking. In the 19th century however relatively cheap glass for roofs became more widely available whilst cast iron as a building material enabled many buildings to be constructed which had not previously been practical. And the availability of gas lighting made it economical to light large buildings artificially for the first time.

Market halls appeared in most major towns during the 19th century and many fine examples still exist.

Sadly many others were destroyed during the second world war or succumbed to developers during the 1960s.

Birkenhead's famous covered market opened on 10th July 1835 on its first site on Market Street opening on Tuesdays and Fridays only. By 1841 the demands posed by the town's burgeoning population meant that the market had to expand.

To meet the increasing needs of the town's shopping public the council bought more land in Hamilton Street in order to build a much larger market. The much celebrated new market hall measured 430 feet by 131 feet. Seven hundred tons of cast iron were used in constructing the new building which was then considered to be of a revolutionary design. At its opening in 1845 the new market hall was illuminated by 92 lamps and featured two large fountains as centrepieces. The new market became well known throughout the North West. It was in the Birkenhead market in 1894 that Michael Marks opened the second of his Penny Bazaars, a market stall which would eventually expand to become the Marks and Spencer's retail empire.

Disaster however lay waiting in the wings. In 1909 a major fire caused extensive damage to the market hall. Sixty five years later another and far worse blaze followed. Almost a hundred firemen were called in to fight the conflagration but to no avail. Although fortunately no-one was injured in the huge blaze the market was completely destroyed by the fire which caused over two million pounds worth of damage.

Below: *Another view of the market in the late 1950s.*

And so the great fire consigned to history part of Birkenhead's cultural heritage. Only in photographs and in the minds eye would we be able to revisit the scene of so many memories. How many of us recall visiting the market as small children accompanying our mothers, fathers and grandparents. Can you remember the confused bustle, smells and noise of within the building; perhaps a little fearful or shy and holding firmly to an adult's hand as we were taken from the cold, wet outdoors into the covered hall and entered a magic kingdom of fishmongers, butchers, booksellers and greengrocers.

To enter the market in those days of childhood was indeed to enter a world which assaulted all the senses and made an indelible impression on young minds: how much were tomatoes per pound in those days? We may not quite remember the cost but we do remember the man who shouted out the price at the top of his voice. It takes less than a second to close one's eyes and recall the extraordinary mixture of aromas that filled the air, an improbable mixture of oranges, soap powder, blood, sawdust, coffee and confectionery, in combination as exotic as any oriental bazaar.

As a result of the fire the market was moved to its present site at the Grange Precinct. The newest new market, the second largest covered market in Britain, was opened on 9th September 1977 - only Leeds' Kirkgate Market is larger.

Today's market, recently refurbished, is home to 347 individual stalls of which 100 are in the outdoor covered section and 247 indoors.

Above the front entrance is the original clock which had once been placed above the 1835 market hall. In 1845 the clock had moved to the market's new home - and would no doubt still have been there had it not crashed to the ground during the 1974 fire.

After the fire the clock was assumed to be lost, taken away as part of the general scrap cleared from the site of the conflagration. The remains of the clock were however later discovered in the corner of a scrapyard by a local newspaper.

A fund was set up to pay for the clock's restoration. Local horological experts were eventually successful in restoring the venerable timepiece to its former glory.

At the very heart of the Wirral, Birkenhead Market sells almost every type of commodity imaginable. The market is a favourite destination for tourists especially coach trips from North Wales attracting more than four and a half million visitors each year. The market now opens six days a week Monday to Saturday between 9 am and 5 pm

Whilst retaining its traditional atmosphere new ideas are also encouraged. In one case both the new and the old have been combined: an idea put into action has been to name the aisles after famous local people. One of them, Dean's Aisle for example is named after the famed Everton footballer Dixie Dean the greatest goal scoring centre forward in football history. Laird's Aisle is named after the Scottish founder of Laird's shipyards which played such an important part in Birkenhead's rise to fame.

The outdoor market is worked on a casual basis and traders are awarded space through a points system. The market is tremendously popular with traders and there is a five year waiting list for indoor stalls. In the last seven years only one stall has come up for sale and then only because the owner had died without leaving a will.

In the long term whatever the future may bring , whatever vagaries in fashion and shopping habits, despite internet shopping and out of town shopping centres somehow markets will survive. Markets, market places and above all market halls have been with us for too long to disappear. As long as there are people to shop there will be those who prefer to do their shopping in a friendly, informal, environment, buying from stall holders who are visibly real folk, rather than in the robotic, impersonal atmosphere of newer venues. Long live the market!

Above: *The market today.*
Left: *The old market clock - back in its rightful place.*

Retail therapy in Birkenhead's Centre

Contrary to some views history did not end with the Second World War. On the contrary, history ended only yesterday. And very soon tomorrow, next week and even next year will be history too.

Modern or recent history is as important, sometimes more important than 'ancient history' because too often it is disregarded and thus forgotten to the point that we know less about what happened a decade or two ago than we do about events which occurred long before we were born.

An important part of every town's history is its architectural landscape. In dynamic, thriving towns that landscape is forever changing and evolving before our eyes - sometimes so quickly that we are shocked that the change has occurred. And sometimes things change so slowly that they are imperceptible until one day we look at what we thought was a familiar location and realise that it no longer bears any resemblance to the place we remember from childhood. The

Grange Shopping Centre is one such example of Birkenhead's changing townscape which, having now been in existence for rather longer than many of us can believe, deserves recognition as part of the town's modern history.

It is in fact now more than thirty years ago that plans were first announced to provide Birkenhead with a brand new shopping centre on Grange Road, surrounding the site of the new Municipal market on three sides.

The company which set out to achieve that commendable objective, helping revitalise the whole area, was a joint venture company made up of three parties: Wirral's own borough council, the Shell Oil Company's pension fund and thirdly, joining those strange bedfellows, the Commissioners of the Church of England. The euphoria and seemingly unstoppable good times of

Above: The newspaper article announcing plans for an extension to the Grange Shopping Centre in the early 1990s. Below: Work begins on the Centre.

GRANGE BILL!

● Extension unveiled ... how the centre may look after the £11m work

EXCLUSIVE by Anne Harrison

DEVELOPERS have revealed £11m extension plans for one of Merseyside's busiest shopping centres.

The extension at Birkenhead's Grange Shopping Centre will include a 25,000sq ft store, a fast food outlet, three new shops and a 500-space multi-storey car park.

Proposed

The scheme, proposed for the Claughton Street end of Princes Pavement, ties in with Wirral City Lands' proposals for a new bus and coach station and parking improvements on the old Asda car park opposite Birkenhead Market.

If Wirral Council grants planning permission next week, work on the extension should begin next summer

Extension plan will cost £11m

and take 12 months to complete.

Legal and General Property, which owns the centre, says the development, particularly the badly-needed extra parking, will benefit the whole town.

Senior assistant manager David Alker added: "The scheme reinforces Legal and General's commitment to the Grange Shopping Centre which we bought two years ago."

He said local people's views would be taken into account and that after comments from market traders, the company intended to improve the pedestrian link between the market and St Werburgh's Square.

Market traders are concerned that there is no direct access to the market from the multi-storey car park and have objected to the plans which go before councillors next week.

They also say the extension will shield the market hall from view and hit trade.

Interfering

Birkenhead Market Traders Association spokeswoman Barbara Arnold said: "They are seriously interfering with pedestrian flow and visibility of the market.

"They are putting up a great big brick wall to stop people seeing us.

"We have 2,000 people working here, making us the town centre's biggest employer. We have already lost jobs in recent years and we don't want to lose any more."

the 1960s had yet to be spoiled by increasing unemployment and runaway inflation of later years and optimism for the new project was high.

Strictly speaking at the time it opened The Grange Shopping Centre was not technically a shopping centre at all but the Grange Shopping Precinct; a

Above: The Centre begins to take shape as building work progresses. Top: St John's Pavement entrance (from Grange Road).

distinction made all the more important by the need to avoid any confusion with the existing shopping area of Grange Road.

In fact the open air and long shopping malls were designed to continue the feel of Grange Road which today runs into the shopping centre via St John's Pavement, St John's Square and beyond.

The first stage of building was not however to be the last. It was in the autumn of 1992 that Legal & General Property bought the centre and announced a major refurbishment and development programme. The proposals were not to change the centre but simply make it a better place to shop.

The first phase of new work however was extensive and would take in the area from WH Smith in St John's Pavement through to St Werburghs Square and part of Princes Pavement, and included the erection of glazed canopies to provide weather protection in the two squares - St John's and St Werburgh's - and large parts of Borough Pavement, Princes Pavement and Milton Pavement.

In the first stage the malls were re-paved with York Stone as well as the addition of decorative paving, installing new street lighting, signage and street

furniture; whilst addressing public anxiety over security a safer environment was assured by installing security cameras and patrolling security guards.

Building a stylish new pavilion in St John's Square provided a focus for special events in the Shopping Centre.

In 1997 the second phase of redeveloping The Grange Shopping Centre began, major building work was undertaken to create a new 500 space multi-storey car park, a new Argos Superstore, a new Yorkshire Bank plus ten further units were added at the north end of Princes Pavement. Before these works began the demolition of the old but historic Argyle Public House had to be undertaken.

Naturally traders as well as customers were concerned about the mess which would ensue from all the work involved. The really messy and difficult work however was done outside normal trading hours to ensure minimum disruption to business. Work started on Monday February 5th in 1995 and was completed in September 1997 and the new Grange Shopping Centre was born.

One consequence of new work was that the pedestrianised areas ceased to be the responsibility of the local council and cleaning and lighting would in future be managed by the owners. Furthermore security, promotional events and charity collections

became a matter for the centre manager to control, who would also put an end to unlawful street trading.

The revamping of the centre was drawn up in consultation with Wirral City Lands, a government and European sponsored organisation which was then planning several new local facilities including the new bus and coach station on adjacent land and a re-modelled car park opposite the market.

Generally the changes were welcomed by Birkenhead traders most believing that improved security for shoppers would add to the town's attractions bringing even more shoppers to the

Above: *Borough Pavement after refurbishment work.*
Top: *St John's Square.*

headed by Norma Clarke the Centre Manager. Norma who is a local Birkonian is well known for her work with local children's charities and her involvement with Birkenhead town centre. Having come from a retail background Norma took up her appointment in May 1993 shortly after the centre was bought by Legal and General.

Since buying the Grange Shopping Centre, Legal and General has now spent some £14 million making improvements. No doubt more changes and more improvements will follow over the coming years. Young people today walking around Birkenhead visiting the shopping centre cannot recall a time when it was not there. For them the buildings have been there literally 'since time immemorial'. To their elders perhaps the buildings however seem new. Both views are wrong. Of all the customers visiting the Grange Shopping Centre time is undoubtedly the slippiest customer of all - tricking young and old alike.

town. Some businesses within the centre, such as Marks and Spencer, took the opportunity to refurbish their own premises to complement those being made to the centre as a whole.

Interestingly at the same time as work began on major improvements to the Grange Shopping Centre other changes were occurring nearby. In April 1995 work began on demolishing the Conway Street flyovers long regarded as the big physical and psychological barrier in the town. The flyovers had been erected in 1967, the old Birkenhead Corporation building in Conway Street having been demolished in order to make way for them.

The concrete roadways were built to take traffic away from Birkenhead town centre but when the Wallasey Tunnel opened they were not used as much. City Challenge development plans in conjunction with Wirral Council put new emphasis on improved links between the Grange Shopping Centre, Hamilton Square and the Woodside business areas. Traffic surveys taken in 1993 showed that the removal of the flyover would have minimal impact on traffic and improve the aspect of the new Conway Park development.

Once the dust of demolition had settled the town centre became much more inviting.

Most of the national multiples are represented in the Grange Shopping Centre's 118 units making it one of the largest shopping centres in the country. The current management team is

The past however really did begin yesterday, and any building more than a quarter of a century old has an indisputable right to proudly consider itself to be part of a town's heritage. Having safely passed the test of having been around for a whole generation the Grange Shopping Centre can surely now honestly lay claim to being part of our, and Birkenhead's, history.

Above: St Werburgh's Square.
Below: The newly opened multi-storey car park.

The treasure of the Pyramids

Mention pyramids to most folk and they will think of Egypt and the great pyramid of Cheops at Giza. On the other hand the French may think of Paris and the modern glass pyramid in the courtyard of the Louvre. For residents of Birkenhead and the Wirral however, the word has more recently become associated with the Pyramids Shopping Centre off Borough Road.

Somewhat younger than the five thousand year old pyramids of Egypt the Pyramids Shopping Centre opened its £25 million doors back in 1989, beginning a whole new shopping era for the people of Birkenhead.

The imaginatively designed scheme provided 160,000 sq ft of prime shopping space for famous retailers such as C&A, Marks & Spencer, Etam, Chelsea Girl, Top Shop, Greenwoods, Dorothy Perkins and Strand Libraries. Thirty five smaller shopping units were also provided.

Linking with the Grange and the town's covered market the Pyramids development created a shoppers' paradise. A major feature of the new centre was its glass lift and escalator entrance while a new 750 space car park was linked to it via a glass-walled pedestrian bridge.

At the heart of the centre is the Pyramid Court, a strikingly designed glass roofed mall cafe seating 120, allowing shoppers to rest in comfort before resuming their shopping sprees.

The idea for the centre had been in existence for many years. Plans were actually drawn up soon after the end of the second world war for

rebuilding war-damaged Birkenhead with a glassed-in shopping precinct. Almost half a century later the planner's dream became a reality as the glass and brick of the Pyramids Centre completed Wirral's showpiece shopping place and finally eliminated the derelict site which had blighted the town centre for so many years.

The Pyramid Shopping Centre was built by Sibec Developments Ltd; building had begun in 1986 with the unimaginative name 'Grange 2'. The name 'the Pyramids' began life simply as a local nickname when part of the building's steel frame took that shape - the building of course bears no serious resemblance to either Egyptian of Aztec pyramids - although since it acquired its name everything has been done to capitalise on the unexpectedly acquired fame.

*Below: Borough Road before the centre. **Bottom left:** An architect's model of the centre. **Bottom right:** The Pyramids during construction.*

Henry E Cotton JP, the Lord Lieutenant of Merseyside, formally opened the new centre in August 1989, rather later than expected. Completion had been delayed by a shortage of glass and bricks.

The centre is built on the banks of what was once Birkenhead's 'Happy Valley', the ancient walk known for its happy atmosphere and a connection which unsurprisingly prompted the developers and others in 1989 to express the hope that shoppers and visitors to the new centre would also find happiness within it precincts. The whole site has a long history: Grange Road for example lies along an old track used by monks in the 12th century leading from their priory to their grange. Borough Road follows the wooded route of the 'Happy

Top: An aerial view of the area, with the Pyramids in the centre. **Right:** *The Pyramids today.*

Valley', but it was not until, the 1830s that Birkenhead started to grow when a market opened there. By the 1870s the town was spreading out from Hamilton Square to Grange Lane - now Grange Road - and shops and stores began appearing in large numbers at the Charring Cross end of the borough turning it into the town's main shopping area.

Since its opening the Pyramids Shopping Centre has done much to ensure that a continuing flow of shoppers are drawn to the area - not least in its first year of opening, when the still-to-be world champion boxer Frank Bruno visited the centre, followed two months later by a spectacular Christmas fireworks display during which Santa Claus arrived by hot air balloon. Since then a regular programme of attractions has been laid on by the management to ensure that visitors remain attracted to the centre.

Whilst Birkenhead may not quite enjoy the hot sunny climate of Cairo, thanks to the Pyramids Shopping Centre mummies and their children visiting this part of the world can at least do their shopping without fear of getting their feet wet. But, more than simply keeping dry, they can be assured of an all round shopping experience in surroundings which would have astonished previous generations.

Ellesmere Port Collection

Making a living

Above: In 1960, when this line of traffic and pedestrians was photographed, it was still a common sight to see people pedalling off to the factory or shipyard. The queue looks like a line of refugees making its way from some battle zone. It was nothing so sinister, just the usual trail across the level crossing by Ellesmere Port Station. The old cattle arch is behind the wall, on the left. WH Wilson's timber yard is on the skyline. It moved to the Rossmere Industrial Estate in April 1965. Also in the distance the Police Station and the National Westminster Bank can be made out. The scooter overtaking the line of cars became one of the symbols of youth later in the 1960s. On their 150cc Lambrettas and Vespas, teenagers paraded around to impress the girls. Nicknamed 'mods', because of their love of modern pop groups such as the Small Faces, they were the arch enemies of 'rockers'. This set rode powerful motorbikes and harked back to the music of Gene Vincent and Eddie Cochran. Clashes between the rivals at Clacton, Brighton and Southsea on Bank Holiday Mondays became the unacceptable face of summer.

Above right: There is rapt attention for this darts match in the Cammell Laird engine shop in 1963. It was probably a lunch break activity, being enjoyed by a group of skilled craftsmen and apprentices. There had been a time when an engineering apprenticeship at Cammell Laird, with its long history of shipbuilding, was much sought after, seeming to

offer a secure future. Undoubtedly, however, times were more uncertain in the later 1950s, with over-capacity in the more traditional areas of shipbuilding. In fact the Chairman of the company himself, Mr Robert Johnson, went on a personal selling mission to Scandinavia in 1964. On the other hand it was not all 'doom and gloom'. In 1961 the launch of the 65,500 ton Royal Dutch Shell tanker, 'Sepia', marked not only the twelfth Shell tanker to have been built at the Cammell Laird yards, but also the largest that the firm had ever built. The government too gave the company a huge boost when, in 1963, the contract to build two nuclear powered Polaris submarines was awarded to Cammell Laird.

Below: Is this man a member of the thought police? He might have been a refugee from the Gestapo with his clipboard, hat and long coat. Whoever he was, he is not helping the flow of traffic into the Mersey tunnel. The trail of vehicles was bumper to bumper in 1955 as it tried to head off into the city. The tunnel had been in operation for just over 20 years. Commuters were happy to wait to enter for a two mile drive that would have been over 10 times longer if they went down the Mersey to the next crossing point. They could have taken the train, but car drivers are a notorious breed. Once the owner of a saloon, never again a passenger on public transport - that was the maxim. It still is now, despite the enormous cost of fuel and the attempts of national and local government to get motorists to break the habit. The Wirral got its first link under the Mersey way back in 1886. The railway opened up both sides of the estuary, encouraging two way commuting and helping our peninsula to grow. As the car became popular, after World War I, it was obvious that a road link had to be established to avoid the long detour. At first, the idea of a bridge was mooted. But, having been successful with one tunnel, it was decided to use that experience and have something similar for cars. Work began in 1925. It was a mammoth project. Ventilation shafts were sunk that towered 200 feet into the sky. Fortunately, the drilling teams from either bank met up, or they might be drilling still!

Bottom: By the look of the smiling faces it's the end of another working day as men pour out of the Cammell Laird yards in 1957. It is interesting to note how many of the older working-men are clad in the traditional flat caps, a 'badge' that was clearly being abandoned by the younger generation. Still, life is all about change, and the decade 1950-1960 saw plenty of that in the Merseyside shipbuilding industry. In one respect it was a time of gathering confidence after the exhaustion and bleakness of the immediate post-war years. The second purpose built 'Ark Royal' aircraft carrier was built and launched at the Cammell Laird yards in 1955, as had the first one in 1937. There was a growth in the building of oil tankers - the emblems of Esso, Shell and BP became familiar sights. Naval contracts included the submarine 'Grampus', in 1957, and the guided missile destroyer, 'Devonshire', in 1960. On the downside, the later 1950s were plagued by bitter industrial demarcation disputes at Cammell Laird. Both sides of the coin were shown in 1959 - the launch of the mighty liner, 'Windsor Castle', along with a prolonged dispute between boilermakers and shipwrights as to who should chalk lines on ships' plates.

Below centre: The Lee Tapestry Works was once an integral part of the Birkenhead industrial scene, but sadly it has been no more than a fond memory for many years. It was in 1888 that Arthur Lee established his first factory, at Warrington, but he transferred his enterprise to Stanley Road, Birkenhead, in 1908. 'The Tapestry', as it was known locally, went from strength to strength in its production of top quality curtain material, chair covering and wall tapestries. The factory employed over 400 people and over half the firm's products were exported, bringing widespread prestige to Birkenhead. The photograph shows one of the employees at work on a Jacquard loom in 1948. Arthur Lee was both an enterprising and an inventive man, for looms like this could only accommodate five colours. He devised a system by which extra colours could be hand-blocked onto the cloth after it had left the loom. As well as machine-woven tapestries, the firm produced hand-embroidered tapestries using crewel embroidery and hand needlework techniques. The wall tapestries were undoubtedly the most prestigious of the Arthur Lee products, especially one huge one that was made for the board room of the Midland Bank. Unfortunately economic pressures forced 'The Tapestry' to close in 1970.

Bottom: Where would this country be without its womenfolk? They feed us, clothe us, do the shopping and juggle the family budget. Clean shirts are ironed and tea is on the table when hubby comes home from work. Just when you think they have done enough, politicians plunge us into another war. When that happened in 1914 it coincided with the women's suffrage movement. Off they went to factories and got behind the wheels of lorries to make sure that the boys at the front were kept supplied and the nation's economy was kept running. When it all began again in 1939, women answered the call. These workers, pictured in the 1920s, were more than ready. Many of those who went into engineering and the heavier industries never left. Once considered too delicate for much more than work in the textile mills, they had proved their worth. When peace came these women had tasted responsibility beyond the kitchen sink. They were not going back to being just housewives. Employers were happy to see them. So many men had not returned from the front. Many of those who had were so badly hurt that they could no longer handle the work they used to. There was an opening in the job market. Women filled it admirably.

chance that enemy agents might mount a land attack. These were the times of revolution abroad. There had been turmoil in Russia and unrest again in Germany. Britain had its own subversives, as well. Another factor to tip the balance was the high cost of building such a bridge. Estimates were put at around £10,000,000. The alternative of a tunnel would be just £6,500,000. For two good reasons, finance and fear, it was the tunnel that received the go ahead. Of all days, it was Christmas Day, 1925 when the first spade went into the ground. The pilot tunnels running from either shore met up 27 months later.

Top: The tunnel, named Queensway in honour of Queen Mary, opened to traffic in 1934. A new tunnel to Wallasey, unimaginatively called Kingsway, opened in 1971. Perched high on the scaffolding, these workers were part of a team building the first road tunnel under the Mersey. It was a tribute to the skill of the architects and engineers who could complete such a major undertaking without the aid of computers to guide them every step of the way. Stretching out as far as they dare, the workforce was making preparations for cement gunning in the main tunnel. One irony of the creation of the tunnel was that all historical information about it had to be moved. The old library was just one of a number of buildings pulled down to make way for the Mersey Tunnel. It is now sited on Borough Road. King George V acknowledged that the name of the road tunnel was a tribute to his wife. He came in person to perform the opening ceremony on 18 July 1934. For good measure, he opened the new Central Library as well. He did not carry out many more official duties. The King passed away the following January. He was well liked for his blunt, straightforward manner. 'I don't like abroad, I've been there' was one of his comments that amused his subjects.

Above: Completing their journey through the Mersey Tunnel in 1934, this line of cars had made the two mile journey from the city under the river for the very first time. It would not be their last. The new access route to and from the Wirral proved immensely successful with everyone. Commuters had an easy journey. Shoppers could get from home to the other side without the need to wait at the station. The tunnel helped to change the pattern of population almost as much as the rail tunnel had done in the previous century. When plans to cross the Mersey were made in the 1920s, the initial idea was to have a bridge. Britain has a history of fine and successful structures like Stephenson's Britannia railway and Telford's road bridges over the Menai Strait. They were engineers of the finest order, part of our heritage. But, the 1914-18 war was still fresh in people's minds. They had seen Zeppelins and the development of the aeroplane. There were real fears that any bridge would be vulnerable to bombing, if there was a return to hostilities. If not from the air, then there was always the

A *leading light*

One of the sights of Ellesmere Port is the night time view of the many lights illuminating Associated Octel's processing plant in the appropriately named Oil Sites Road. In 1948 the 60 acre site for a new tetra-ethyl lead or 'TEL' plant to be built by the Associated Ethyl Company Ltd was chosen at Ellesmere Port in Cheshire. In fact it practically chose itself. The site bordered the Manchester Ship Canal and Shell, one of the company's major customers, was about to expand its refinery literally next door. The main chemical 'intermediates', including sodium ethyl chloride and ethylene dichloride were also to be made at the new Ellesmere Port facility.

Building work began in 1951. Construction costs had been estimated at £11 million. In the end the cost doubled. One reason was inflation, a second was the sheer size and complexity of the task. The money was found from the company's shareholders. Another difficulty, apart from escalating costs was the post war rationing of steel which held up construction for several months. In the end the government gave approval to import 4,000 tons of steel to add to the 2,500 tons already allocated through the rationing scheme.

The statistics relating to the plant at Ellesmere Port were impressive. There were 200,000 square yards of timber used on construction - enough to cover 20 football pitches; 100,000 cubic yards of concrete were used. 7,000 foundation piles were made necessary by the fact that the site had previously been marshland. 5,000,000 bricks were used, enough to build 200 houses. Up to 4,000 construction workers were brought in from south Lancashire, Merseyside and Manchester. More than 4,000 drawings and plans were made by Associated Ethyl's own Engineering Design Group which took responsibility for the whole project. Construction was complete and full scale production begun in 1954.

But where did Octel come from and what on earth is TEL? Today's Associated Octel Company Ltd began its corporate life in September 1938 as the Associated Ethyl Company. Its joint owners were the world's six major oil companies: Shell, Exxon, BP, Mobil, Texaco and Chevron together with General Motors. Keeping a

Above: *The Octagon, first of the company's in-house magazines.* ***Below:*** *Workers in 1945.*

close eye on developments, and the only customer however, was the British government which considered the company's product to be an essential strategic supply in the event of war - and how right they were!

When the second world war began the government's wisdom in helping establish Associated Ethyl was soon demonstrated. The company made TEL or tetra-ethyl lead, an octane enhancing fuel additive which dramatically improved engine performance. With TEL in their fuel tanks Hurricanes and Spitfires could fly faster, further and higher. Following the war Air Chief Marshal Bomber Harris said that much effort could have been spared if allied bombers had targeted the enemy chemical plants making TEL rather than the many scattered fuel dumps.

In addition to increasing power TEL also made engines more efficient, have a longer life and require less maintenance and emit fewer emissions; it also improved fuel consumption by 15 per cent.

Above: *The Ellesmere Port site in the early 1950s. The steel used to construct the plant was enough to build several Blackpool Towers.*

The discovery of TEL, the 'lead' in leaded petrol, was made in 1918 by an American, Thomas Midgely junior, the head of research at General Motors who set out to find a way of reducing 'knocking' or 'pinking'. Combined with other compounds to oxidise unwanted deposits TEL became the main constituent of the complete compound known simply as 'Ethyl'. In 1923 Ethyl was sold for the first time as a fuel additive. The new chemical was at first sold separately at filling stations to discerning motorists. By 1926 however Ethyl was been added routinely to petrol before delivery to filling stations. By the end of the war, by contrast, almost 100% of petrol was leaded.

Another strategic product was chlorine. In 1952 ICI had warned the government that it could not guarantee supplies beyond 1957. There being no other suitable suppliers Associated Ethyl's Design Group set to work on a mercury cell chlorine plant for Ellesmere Port which would be complete by 1958. Fascinatingly, surplus hydrogen (a by-product) would be piped seven miles to the Unilever plant to help make margarine. In the year the new chlorine plant was completed the company installed its first computer at Ellesmere Port, an 'English Electric' model: those were the days.

The name Octel first appeared as a brand name in 1954 to distinguish the product from the US firm's Ethyl. By 1956 Octel was the world's largest producer of TEL supplying 70 per cent of all refineries outside of North America. It was not however until 1961 that the company changed its name to the Associated Octel Company Ltd, by which time a comprehensive range of nine different lead-based anti-knock compounds were being manufactured.

By the early 1960s environmental issues were beginning to come to the fore. At Ellesmere Port total containment vessels were fitted to fifteen autoclaves to guard against unwanted discharges. New effluent treatment facilities were also installed whilst carbon absorbers and electrostatic precipitators reduced airborne emissions.

A cloud appeared on the company's horizon in 1966 when California introduced legislation to reduce car exhaust emissions. Similarly, legislation has since been introduced in other countries across the world. The intention was to reduce the amount of unburnt hydrocarbons, nitrogen oxides and carbon monoxide emitted by cars which were contributing to urban smog and global warming. The solution was the fitting of catalytic converters to vehicles. Sadly for the company such converters only work in the absence of lead and so Octel was faced with a serious challenge. Interestingly in 1980 a British Government report into lead pollution concluded that the main sources of lead in the human body were food and water and not as was commonly thought from atmospheric lead from car

exhausts: but that did not change the outcome. In 1983 the Government introduced a timetable for the introduction of unleaded petrol in the UK.

By 1992 the world market for anti-knock compounds had fallen by 80 per cent, down from almost a million tonnes a year in 1973 to 200,000. By 1997 the figure had halved again.

New products were needed to fill the commercial gap. A new ethyl chloride plant had already come on stream

Above: *This reach-stacker was acquired for Ellesmere Port in 1992 and can lift loads of up to 40 tonnes.* ***Top:*** *A total containment vessel edging slowly to Ellesmere Port.*

at Ellesmere Port in the 1970s and a new cell hall at the chlorine works had increased production by fifty per cent.

Another plant opened in 1988 to produce a detergent fuel additive. Demand for that new product soon boosted Octel's status as a major supplier of non-lead fuel additives to both refineries and chemical companies.

In 1989 control of the company passed to the Great Lakes Chemical Corporation (GLCC). Investment in Ellesmere Port continued, including spending £8.5 million on the installation of mercury free membrane cells in the chlorine works, an initiative which substantially reduced the space required. The space released, valued at £1.45 million, was used to build a new £9 million chemical plant.

Meanwhile the drive to be environmentally responsible had continued and major emissions and discharges at the site were reduced by 80 per cent during the course of the 1990s.

In 1997 GLCC decided on a demerger, giving Octel corporate independence. The 'new' Octel company would consist of the Ellesmere Port complex, a Fuel Technology Centre in Bletchley, Octel America Inc in the USA and a London office. The demerger occurred in May 1998.

> *In May 1998 Octel was given corporate independence with a demerger*

Today Octel is a growing speciality chemicals company. It continues to supply TEL to those customers worldwide who still need it. Under its product stewardship programme, the company provides customers with a complete package of 'clean up' services, from decommissioning and decontamination to sludge removal and reprocessing. The company is now also selling many new products, not only in non-lead fuel additives but also a growing number of other chemicals.

Non-lead fuel additives sales have increased from six million pounds in 1990 to over 35 million pounds today with a potential market of over £500 million.

Octel products are being developed for many different uses: household detergents, paper and textile manufacture, water treatment, metal processing, oil production and a host of other applications from photography to plastics and inks.

Despite the demise of leaded petrol there can be little doubt that the twinkling lights of the Octel plant are still destined to shine just as brightly for many years to come.

Below: *The specially adapted Essi Anne at sea.*

One man's vision - **Kingsmead School**

Dominus Vitae Robur - The Lord is the strength of life

Kingsmead School was founded in 1904 by Arthur Watts, one of six brothers, five of whom would play a part in the life of the school. Arthur was a Christian, from a family with a strong Baptist tradition; he was also a Cambridge scholar, a gifted mathematician, who was a 24th Wrangler (no 24 in the first class honours list in all Cambridge). He was also a fine sportsman, notably in rowing and cricket.

Arthur had the academic world at his feet, but preferred to look to the Mission field for his future. However, he decided to gain some secular experience first and took a teaching job in Chester at Arnold House (now part of the King's School). During this time he discovered he had a gift for teaching and realised it was God-given; his youth work with the Scripture Union and Seaside Missions for Children led him to discover West Kirby and

Hoylake, which were not quite as we see them today. In those days Hoylake was a fishing village; you could see the fleet going out, and there were barrows on the streets selling fresh fish. It was a magical place for children, with pine trees and golden sand dunes rising to 50 or 60 feet, clear sea water to bathe in and even its very own smugglers' cottage *(above)*.

Arthur was a man of great simplicity and singlemindedness and in time he resolved to create a school of his own, one in which the environment would be ideal for learning well, for playing good games and keeping physically fit. Above all, he wanted a school where he could develop Christian character. Arthur Watts

loved his Bible; it was the cornerstone of all his character training. By 1904, at the age of 33, he was ready to launch out on his own; the advertisement in the Birkenhead News Wednesday 21st September 1904 announced, *'A new school to be opened in September. The aim will be to give a thoroughly good education, and to develop in the boys a manly Christian character'.*

He started with eight boys at a property on Birkenhead Road, Hoylake. Meanwhile the school building was being constructed on fields adjacent, a few yards down Bertram Drive. Within two years there were 36 boys, of whom 12 were boarders and a large area had been added to the field by rental, making five acres of playing fields in all.

It was in 1907 that the first Kingsmead excursion to climb Moel Famau in north Wales took place. This tradition continues today when in July the whole school from Year 3 (age seven) upwards, set out to 'climb the mountain'.

Above: A school trip to Moel Famau in 1920.
Below: An advertisement from 1911 shows that the school had grown to include 'the big school room', a single-storey extension to a new gable end.
Below left: Boys playing cricket at Kingsmead, 1905.

Above: The 'Huts' - site of the proposed new Junior Department building.

Throughout the decades of the 20th century the school continued to expand and flourish. There were many changes and developments - becoming a Preparatory School, (teaching only to age 13 - 1920s), taking in girls (1960s) - but by far the most significant was in 1966 when the Watts family gave the school to a charitable trust. The Headmaster at the time was Mr David Watts, Arthur's son and successor (with his brother Gordon), from 1949. David wanted to ensure the continuation of the work started by his father, before he himself retired in 1979.

Since then the school has had three Headmasters, but some things have remained constant; a strong Christian education, the influence of the Watts family (through their presence on the Governing body), the same building and even classrooms (the 'Big School Room' is still in use today as a form room). And then there is the lovely site with

Infant, Junior and Senior departments adjacent to each other, its open outlook across farmland and even the original cricket pavilion!

Boarding has been a funda-mental part of the Kingsmead ethos and it continues to flourish today. During the late 1990s numbers have risen steadily as pupils take advantage of Kingsmead's flexible family boarding policy - staying full-term, weekdays or only for the occasional sleepover. Kingsmead is now the only Boarding and Day school left in the Merseyside region.

Educating children from the age of two (*above*) and up to 16 (Key Stage 4 and GCSE), in the year 2000, is no less demanding than when Arthur Watts set out to establish his school in the early years of the 20th century. The same values are just as important; what has changed are the amenities necessary to deliver a broad education for the individual. Kingsmead has retained small class sizes and a highly qualified and well motivated staff, believing these to be the cornerstones of a first-class education tailored to meet the needs of each child.

To provide many of the facilities at Kingsmead, the school has needed to rely on the generosity of generations of parents and past pupils; the same is true today. Recently the Governors launched the Centenary Projects Appeal to raise funds for a new Junior Department building to be erected on the site of the old 'huts'. This appeal is being supported by both many past pupils and staff, as well as today's generation of parents. As the school looks towards its Centenary celebrations in the year 2004, Kingsmead is sure of what it is doing and where it is going; that has not changed and will not change.

Acknowledgments

We are grateful to Mrs Dorothy Watts for her permission to use extracts from her book, 'The Story of Kingsmead', in this article.

Top left: The senior boys boarding cottage.
Below: The main school building - Summer 2000.

No *washday blues for this laundry*

Even when George Formby was singing about the Chinese laundry blues, Mr Woo and that lamppost he used to lean on, the message was one of early automation and the first designs of the household appliances we would recognise today. But, laundries had been around a lot longer than the 1930s and 1940s when old George was at his peak. One such business is still going strong, well over a century after it first opened its doors in West Kirby as a family run business. Deeside Laundry has even tripled its turnover since 1990. It is by far and away the largest such company on the Wirral, with a turnover in excess of £1 million. Its fleet of vans covers an area as far afield as Wrexham and Manchester. The present management of David Cross (chairman) and his wife Anne (company secretary) were able to oversee the opening of a new processing plant in Hoylake in 1998 that deals with all the contract workwear business. Their sons, Jonathan and Nicholas, will be able to share in a successful and fast expanding company, should they join forces with their parents in the future.

Lifestyles and the expectations of the public were far different when Major James Patterson founded the company in 1889.

Above: Richard Armstrong Grier, grandson of the founder. Below: Deeside Laundry in the early 1900s.

Those were the days of stiffly starched petticoats, high collars and long dresses that swept the floor better than any brush. They were grimy days in Victorian industrial Britain. Huge factory chimneys belched out smoke and shirt cuffs did not stay crisp and white for very long in that atmosphere. Housemaids and kitchenmaids in the large mansions had an awful job hand washing and scrubbing in an effort to present their masters and mistresses with fresh, clean linen. When the West Kirby laundry opened, it was a godsend for them, as well as the proprietors of tea shops, restaurants and other businesses that needed a prompt and efficient service. Victorian laundries used huge dollies and tubs, but it was all a hand operation. Flat irons, heated on large ranges, were put the knife edge creases in garments that had been brought in on a horse and cart and were sent back the same way, as good as new.

Major Patterson sold the laundry to his brother in law, Matthew Grier in 1890. This was the start of a connection with several generations of the Grier family that was to continue for nearly 80 years. During one period, there were seven members of the Grier family all holding executive positions. By 1912, the business had prospered to the extent that it was able to expand to the present site in Groveside. The house on the site was extended and became both the living quarters for the Griers and their place of work. The building was full of dolly tubs and wicker baskets as trade boomed and the laundry filled to overflowing. At its height, in those horse drawn days, there were 50 people working for Deeside Laundry.

Above (both pictures): *The Laundry today.*
Right: *Paul Keaney, left, David Cross, centre and Simon Deere outside the firm's additional premises.*

After world War II, electrical appliances became all the rage, both in the home and on the High Street. Launderettes had first appeared in America in the 1930s. They crossed the Atlantic 20 years later. These, and the electrical twin tubs, driers and washers that entered every housewife's kitchen, meant that change was on the way. In 1968, the laundry was sold to Joseph Cross, father of the current chairman. He had run the County Laundry in North Wales. The majority of the work would now come from industrial sources as the laundry's business approach was reshaped. This process has been continued by David Cross and his management team as they take Deeside Laundry further into the 21st century as a successful and thriving company.

Instead of dealing with the 'tweenies' or 'below stairs' staff of the Victorian houses, Deeside Laundry now works with restaurants, hotels, factories and garages. Modern fabrics need complex equipment and processes to remove the ingrained grease and grime with which they are faced from thousands of garments each week. The laundry still deals with the general public, offering a same day dry cleaning service. But, it is the challenges presented by the changing needs of industry that will keep Deeside Laundry busy and successful for many years to come.

Lighting up a century

In the first year of the twentieth century Queen Victoria died and was succeeded by her son King Edward VII, the former Prince of Wales and first gentleman of the Empire. In the USA President William McKinley was assassinated by an anarchist and succeeded by Theodore Roosevelt.

In South Africa the Boers had begun the third year of their guerrilla war against the British in their ultimately unsuccessful attempt to establish the independence of the Transvaal, whilst in Peking the Boxer rebellion drew to a close. And in Birkenhead a small firm of electricians made its tentative start in life.

The Prenton firm of James Heaney & Co Ltd was founded in 1901 by James W Heaney. James took over from his father Jack Heaney who already had premises in Borough Road Birkenhead since the late 19th century from which he had worked as an electrician.

James Heaney took over from his father, who was already an established electrician in the town

Electricity was then still a relatively new idea, at least to the man in the street. The electric light bulb invented by Swann in England and Thomas Edison in the USA was still only a few years old and whilst the wealthy may have been able to afford for their houses to be wired, few ordinary folk could afford such a luxury, content to continue with gas lighting - and the less fortunate with oil lamps. Indeed, so common was gas lighting that most of the early electricians were also plumbers, the move from water through to gas and finally to electricity being a natural progression of the trade.

Although the business began as a general electricians it quickly came to specialise in the brewery trade after obtaining a contract to wire the Birkenhead brewery to the mains system.

Below: *The company's Prenton premises.*

When James Heaney died in 1955 his death was quickly followed by not only that of his wife but also his partner Charlie McDonald an event which left Jim Pinnington entirely on his own.

The Borough Road premises continued to be used by the firm until the 1920s when the still small firm moved to premises in Woodchurch Road. Those premises were to be used by the firm for over forty years, until 1967, when another move was made, this time to the present business premises in Prenton Road West, the building having previously been a branch office of the Midland Bank.

For over fifty years James Heaney persevered with his business, seeing it through the years of the Great War, the boom which followed, hard times of the 1920s, the depression years of the 1930s and the shortages of men and materials during the second world war. After the ending of World War II the firm could at last look forward to a degree of prosperity in the post war boom which would follow.

Sadly James Heaney, the firm's founder, died in 1955; he was the last and only member of the Heaney family to be involved but his two partners - Jim Pinnington, who during the war had been in the Royal engineers and served overseas, and Charles MacDonald - carried on the company.

This page: *New floodlighting for Tranmere Rovers.*

Fortunately Jim Pinnington's two sons later joined the firm. Jim Pinnington junior and his brother Cyril later became directors alongside their father, together with Charles Bridges (who was Company Secretary) until their retirement.

Ron Lawrence had started working for the company in 1953 and 1989 bought Cyril Pinnington's shares when Cyril in turn retired.

In 1992 Tonny Kerkhofs joined the firm as contracts manager and in 1997 Ron Lawrence and Tonny Kerkhofs bought Jim Pinnington's share in the firm on Jim junior's retirement. Today Ron Lawrence is chairman and managing director whilst Tonny Kerkhofs is the firm's commercial director.

A considerable amount of work was once done in the docks by the firm. Main customers of the firm in recent years however have included providing floodlighting and new stand electrics for Tranmere Rovers, West Kirby Residential School for Children with Special Needs and the Stanley Casinos whilst the car tyre and exhaust firm Kwik- Fit are major customers throughout the North West and Wales.

Today, with its staff, of 12 the company can undertake almost any domestic, industrial or commercial job.

Chairman Ron Lawrence is now looking to retire in the next couple of years Tonny Kerkhofs however intends to carry on well beyond the company's centenary celebrations.

From little acorns...

As a nation whose economy was once built upon the farming that was rural England, it is no surprise that we still turn to the land for a lot of our recreation. From allotments to tiny window boxes, the average Briton puts his hands into the good Lord's earth as often as did his ancestors. It has been said that angling is the nation's most popular sport, but gardening must be the biggest pastime. Every weekend backs are bent, weeds pulled and tender bedding plants carefully nurtured. Tomatoes are fed and rows of potatoes earthed up. For an industrial and technological society, we are remarkably good at returning to nature for our enjoyment.

The growth in garden centres that cater for every need, from the humblest packet of Webb's Wonderful lettuce seeds through to the finest pergolas, has been nothing short of remarkable over the last 30 years. There were always smaller outlets, but this field has become big business and a real growth industry in both senses! Garden centres now include exotic species of plants, summerhouses for sale and refreshment facilities that would have been a pipedream for the old timers who just sold cuttings, John Innes compost and pea sticks.

At the forefront of the Wirral's gardening revolution is the Gordale Nursery & Garden Centre. Situated on Chester High Road, Burton, it occupies 20 acres and includes its own petrol station. All this was made possible from an original five acre site as neighbouring properties were bought up over the years. As with most successful businesses, it now seems hard to imagine the small beginnings from which Gordale came.

Below: *The Nurseries in the 1950s. Peter Nicholson is pictured as a child with his mother.*
Bottom: *Construction of the Nurseries.*

Albert and Gladys Whittaker had set up home in Hoylake in 1925, buying Davies's Dairies which they ran until 1948. By then, their daughter Joyce had married the boy next door, Harold Nicholson. Joyce's mother had died and her father was remarried to Lilian, who had come to the area from the city on health grounds. together, the Whittakers and the Nicholsons took over the smallholding that was to grow into the Gordale Nursery & Garden Centre. At first, the two couples shared the small house that came with the business, as profit margins after the war were tight. It was a market garden that concentrated on vegetable growing. It was as famous for its cafe as its produce. People came specially for its chicken salads. Rationing meant that they could get the sort of meal there that they could not get at home. However, the family was getting frustrated. It was decided to put the property up for auction as the investment was showing little return. Canada, in 1950, seemed to be a land of opportunity.

Plans to emigrate were well in hand when the smallholding was auctioned. It failed to reach its reserve price by just £250. Harold was convinced that the main bidder would put in a revised offer the following day. That was the best mistake he ever made. No-one returned and the tickets to Prince George in the Rockies were cancelled. The family soldiered on and were rewarded by the boom in car ownership. The passing trade increased as families were liberated from their own backyards by the petrol engine. Trade picked up and Gordale Nursery & Garden Centre prospered.

Above: *The Nurseries today from the air...*
Right: *...and the ground.*

The Nicholson's son, Peter, joined the firm in the mid 1970s, having studied horticulture in England and the Netherlands. His wife, Jill, gave up teaching to became a director in the early 1990s. Peter has been able to bring new ideas and a modern redirection to the company that continues to blossom, as all good gardens and centres should. Gordale now employs over 50 staff, plus weekend workers, many having been with the company for a good 20 years. Some refuse to say exactly how long! It is well known for its friendly and knowledgeable service, Peter and Jill practise what they preach and are often seen out and about in the centre, either serving customers or chatting to them about their gardens over a cuppa in the coffee shop. As the number of TV gardening programmes shows, interest in the subject has never been higher. It has never been better served than at Gordale.

Acknowledgments

The publishers would like to thank
Birkenhead Central Library
Cheshire County Council, Archives & Local Studies
Liverpool Libraries & Information Services
Oxton Studios

Thanks are also due to
Peter Thomas and Andrew Mitchell who penned the editorial text and
Steve Ainsworth for his copywriting skills